About the author

Beppe Severgnini is 34 and was born in Crema, near Milan in Italy. He came to Britain for the first time in 1971 and in spite of a few skin-heads chasing him around on the Channel coast, thought it an interesting place. He has come back every year since then.

He has a degree in international law from Pavia University and has been working for *Il Giornale*, a national Italian newspaper, since 1982. In 1984 he was posted to London, and until 1988 he travelled the country, journeying from a basement flat in Notting Hill to such far-flung places as Brighton and the Outer Hebrides. He also managed to visit Liverpool several times without the help of an interpreter.

Now a special political correspondent, he has covered the Middle East, the Beijing riots in 1989 and most of the revolution in Eastern Europe. He still thinks Britain is the most demanding place, matched only by China. 'In both countries,' he wrote, 'there is a strong government, lousy weather and people smile a lot, but they don't give a damn about you.'

He lives in Milan with his wife, Ortensia. *Inglesi* was published by Rizzoli in 1990, was a bestseller in Italy and was reprinted four times.

Inglesi

Beppe Severgnini

CORONET BOOKS
Hodder and Stoughton

Copyright © 1990 RCS Rizzoli Libri S.p.A., Milano

First published in Great Britain in 1991 by Coronet Books

A Coronet Books Original

British Library C.I.P.

Severgnini, Beppe
 Inglesi.
 I. Title
 305.82

 ISBN 0-340-55349-9

Printed and bound in Great Britain for Hodder and Stoughton Paperbacks, a division of Hodder and Stoughton Ltd, Mill Road, Dunton Green, Sevenoaks, Kent TN13 2YA. (Editorial Office: 47 Bedford Square, London WC1B 3DP) by Clays Ltd, St Ives plc. Photoset by Rowland Phototypesetting Ltd, Bury St Edmunds, Suffolk

For Ortensia, who came along

Translated by Paola Pugsley

I wish to thank Indro Montanelli who sent me to London and called me back home in time, and Mr and Mrs Angelo Severgnini who never complained. I wish to thank my colleagues at *Il Giornale*: Gianni Biazzi Vergani, editor-in-chief; Sandra Artom, features editor, and all the foreign editors from Michele Sarcina to Alfredo Pallavisini. I am indebted to my English friends who patiently answered my questions: Melanie Davies; Peter Grimsdale, the pink flamingo; Rose Barker; Caroline Stacey; Charles Hodgson; Nicky Fox; Libby Savill; Ronnie Payne; Stephanie Calman and many more. Many colleagues spent long evenings with me dissecting the Englishman as if he were an insect: I am grateful to all of them and in particular to Michele Calcaterra and Mino Vignolo. Some of the people who helped, like Alessandro Vaciago, Massimo Crovetto, Lino Mannocci and Silvio Marchetti are anglophiles; some, whose names I will not mention, are anglophobes: their punishment is to be lucky enough to live in London. Finally, Mrs Margaret Hilda Thatcher née Roberts: thanks to her there was never a dull moment during my four year stay in the United Kingdom.

Foreword

There is only one real problem with Great Britain. Foreigners land full of preconceived ideas: the British are not very communicative, they love tradition, they read a lot, but don't wash too much. And after a few days the visitor realises all this is absolutely correct: the shock is so great that any further investigation is impossible. But my feeling is that the late twentieth-century Englishman is still uncharted territory, well worth exploring. And so is the land he inhabits.

For a start there are a few things to bear in mind: no nation in the world consists of just its capital city, therefore Britain is not London. In a country of such diversity and size, many people matter in the decision-making process, though we might have had the impression that in the past eleven years only one person did. Things we think we are familiar with, such as black taxi cabs or the Royal Family, are constantly changing. Let's not forget some less obvious, but equally fascinating, aspects of the British social scene: the complex class structure, the depressing coastline, the eccentricities of the 'young fogeys' – trying hard to be old at the age of twenty, the greyhounds and the extravaganza of the 'season' with Wimbledon, Ascot and picnics at Glyndebourne which is when the British pretend they have a summer like everybody else.

I can assure the reader that the exploration is worth the trouble, but it is hard work. Sixty years ago an English travel writer, E. R. P. Vincent, showed great insight with these few words: 'Italia is not Italy.' Italy for him meant the country frozen in time and full of Botticellis and pergolas which generations of English writers had described before him with tears in their eyes. 'Italia,' he went on, 'has a future,

Italy does not, it only has a scant present and an immense past. Italia has bitter icy winds, Italy basks in perennial sunshine. Italia is a strange, hard, throbbing land, Italy is accessible, straightforward and very dead'. We can apply the same approach to Great Britain: the parks, the red buses, the policemen, they always look the same, but there is another nation worth exploring with its silent suburbs and unsettled minorities, nouveaux riches and old habits.

I am not setting out to write a tourist guide. My intention is to provide some information about the British people, how they have fared in the last ten years, how they have coped with an unexpected Prime Minister, and how they have dramatically changed in such a short time. I also intend to praise them; they have understood that a great imperial past is not enough, and today they are better off as good neighbours of Europe. Some people have not got the message, and I'll say so as well. Occasionally I may not take the British too seriously, but I'm sure they don't mind: they have done the same with the rest of the world for centuries.

Like any writer I have my illusions: I would like this book to be of use to anyone who crosses the Channel (above or underneath) on a study trip, on business, or just to buy woollens. And, who knows, perhaps the British themselves, looking at their image in the book, might discover that they are more interesting than they ever suspected.

Beppe Severgnini

I

Where is Great Britain going?

Thanks to Nanny Thatcher

In Great Britain the eighties were the years of Margaret Thatcher, just as much as the sixties belonged to the Beatles. This is not meant to be disrespectful, either to Beatles fans or to Mrs Thatcher's admirers. She has, just like the lads from Liverpool, left an everlasting mark on the country, and the British remember her with a mixture of admiration and horror. One thing is certain: she won't be forgotten all that quickly.

In November 1990, at the time of the leadership contest between John Major, Douglas Hurd and Michael Heseltine, a group of nine-year-old schoolchildren wrote to a newspaper with the following question: 'Can a Prime Minister be a man?' John Major, the son of a circus acrobat, has been in office for too short a time for us to assess whether he will go down in history at all. Some of his predecessors have been easily forgotten: Lord Callaghan's main claim to fame, for instance, is that he made the use of cats' eyes in the middle of the road compulsory.

Margaret Hilda Thatcher, née Roberts, on the other hand, is of the same stock of great leaders as Churchill and the first Queen Elizabeth. Both courageous and hyperactive, she has left a lasting impression on British post-war history. This is not a mere reflection of the long span of time that she was in office, but of the way she went about it. After six years of Harold Wilson, there was no 'Wilsonism': things were just a trifle more chaotic. Four years of the Heath Government did not produce any 'Heathism': it looked more like a last ditch attempt to prop up a collapsing country. Margaret Thatcher had only been in the job three months, and Thatcherism was already there. And still is, some would say.

In 1979 Mrs Thatcher took Britain by storm: in the following twelve years her approach didn't change much. She started her revolution by tackling the 1980–82 recession her way. Instead of stimulating demand, according to the prevailing economic theories, she confronted public spending and inflation head on, disregarding unemployment figures as a temporary, necessary evil. She stated loudly and clearly that wealth had to be created before being distributed: this was the job of private citizens, the State taking the back seat and allowing them more freedom and responsibility.

In Italy, a country where prime ministers change with the seasons, we were flabbergasted by this leader who clearly intended to go down in history. In Britain the shock was such that her opponents are just coming round now. To their horror, the Labour Party realised that she intended not only to thrash them on any occasion, but wanted to convert them. A number of Conservatives could not believe that they had elected her and longed for Disraeli and his 'caring society'. The electors voted her into office three times (1979, 1983 and 1987) and, come to think of it, never fired her.

As we know, Conservative MPs turfed her out of Number 10 and only time will tell whether they were right or wrong. She was certainly authoritarian, hardhearted and possibly stood up too noisily for Britain, but it is only fair to say that she has been the only Prime Minister who had the guts to face the nation with some hard facts. First, and foremost, that Great Britain had won the war on paper, but lost it in practice. By 1945 the country was poor and exhausted: no longer a world power, it had to become something else. With her no-nonsense attitude, Nanny Thatcher forced the country to face reality. She also taught it that there was nothing shameful in competing with South Korea in the production of cutlery; that it did make good economic sense to encourage the working classes to own their own homes, it was not an abomination as Labour said and that it was ludicrous not to stand up to the Trade Unions, when you had beaten the Nazis.

The results of eleven years of Thatcherism are there for everyone to see. Nowadays Great Britain is a modern, reasonably settled and fairly wealthy nation. It has left its former empire behind without abandoning it: the Commonwealth Heads of State still pose with Buckingham Palace in the background, when in London. This new role was a deliberate choice: the Argentinian generals, who got it wrong, found their punishment in the icy waters of the Falklands.

The turning point was the winter of discontent, 1978–79. At a time when, because of the strikes, the dead could not be buried and electricity was rationed, Mrs Thatcher was quick to capitalise on the changing mood of the nation and set out to declare that middle class values, which happened to be her own, were going to be the values for the whole nation. They were: private enterprise, law and order, and national pride. The manifesto turned out to be a vote winner: unlike most politicans, Mrs Thatcher, for ten years at least, was able to preach what she believed in. And her beliefs sold well to the electorate, three times running.

As early as 1975, when Margaret Thatcher became leader of the Conservative Party, the trained student of politics could have detected the signs of the approaching tornado. In the words of one of the losers of the leadership contest, talking of the first meeting of the shadow cabinet (Labour was then in power), 'As she touched up her hair and hooked her bag on the back of the chair, we had the foreboding of impending calamity'. An accurate prophecy: the Tory Party, as Macmillan and Heath had known it, was doomed. Over fifteen years, she altered it beyond recognition, wooing her own lower middle class and ignoring the traditional élite. They maintained they could not stand her, but they loved her after a fashion, like the nobility of old and their stewards: they may not have been pleasant fellows, but they had to be employed and were useful.

The three main parties these days like to think that they are classless, but it is not so. The Labour Party still targets mainly the working class and young people looking for social justice while they are waiting for better paid jobs. Paddy Ashdown's Liberal Democrats get as far as attracting some discontented intellectuals and a few excentrics. Only the new Conservative Party – transformed by the grocer's daughter and handed over to the trapeze artist's son – has taken the plunge. As it is aware that the upper class where it originated from, is numerically limited, it takes votes wherever it can find them.

One does not have to go far to see it. Admittedly at Smith Square, in Conservative Central Office, the perfectly groomed and elegantly bejewelled secretaries could have been kidnapped at a ball, but it is not so elsewhere in Britain. Take Ealing, a London suburb. There I watched Harry Greenway, the Conservative candidate at the last general election. He looked nothing like an aristocrat, and neither did he talk like one. His electors had only secondhand cars, but they were former council tenants having bought their homes thanks to a piece of Conservative legislation, or OAPs at odds with Labour over law and order, or Pakistani shopkeepers delighted to hear Mrs Thatcher preach: make money and your bank account will make you equal.

In Liverpool, a group of party stalwarts has opened a tearoom called 'Thatcher's', where it is possible to indulge in the most British of pastimes, under the gaze of the former Prime Minister. The success of this initiative has shown, according to the organisers, firstly that the sight of Margaret

Thatcher does not spoil your appetite and, secondly, that private enterprise pays, whatever the opposition may say. The place seats about twenty-five people at a time and you will not find any sign of the landed gentry there. Management and customers alike are from the middle class. They believe in looking after themselves and think that the problems of the North of England cannot all be laid at the Government's door.

In the City, a complete contrast with the slums of Liverpool, prayers are uttered daily to keep the Conservatives in power; hardly surprising, but not entirely due to self interest. Since 1979 when Labour were defeated, restrictions on the movement of capital have been abolished, corporate tax reduced, trade unions tamed, and the value of the pound propped up with a ruthless use of interest rates. The City also anticipates that in the single European market to come, Britain will be the main supplier of financial services. No wonder the City loves Europe at least as much as it loves the Tories.

But even those Britons who admired Mrs Thatcher for having turned the country round, had little affection for her. She did not look vulnerable and capable of indulging in harmless peccadillos like the average person, a feeling which the man in the street found unsettling. And not just that: Mrs Thatcher delighted in looking stern and tough even when she was not (as during the rounds of public spending cuts, which at the end of the day were not so drastic): 'After years of self indulgence, the country needs rigorous and harsh treatment: I will see to it,' she would say. Such attitudes earned her many detractors, and a string of ferocious nicknames. I would mention a few: the Westminster Ripper (of obvious origin); 'She who must be obeyed'; 'TBW' which stands for 'That Bloody Woman', and Bossette (this last attributed to Lord Carrington, former Secretary General of NATO). There is also TINA, the brilliant acronym for 'There Is No Alternative' (that's what she used to say when she wanted to cut short a discussion).

The Grantham grocer's daughter knew all this and remained unruffled. Apparently convinced of her own infallibility, she bulldozed her way on, taking no notice of the moaning and groaning behind her back. She never consorted with the aristocracy, a mere tourist asset in her judgement, nor with the academic establishment. Each class repaid her in kind: the aristocracy with admiration, hatred and fear. Oxford University, where she graduated, by publicly denying her an honorary degree, and the newly appointed Knights (journalists, businessmen, and a few trade unionists) with total devotion.

There is no doubt that Great Britain after Mrs Thatcher, like France after de Gaulle, will never be the same. The Iron Lady scared the wits out of the British, and at the end of the day the British admire people they are scared by. Thanks to her rough remedies, millions of them want to compete again or at least are getting their self confidence back, a complete reversal after the seventies. So, badly dressed and fed even worse, the British are now ready to face history and perhaps Europe. Even those who could not stand her (and were denied the satisfaction of voting her out of office) know deep down that she is an outstanding figure. But of course they will never say so in so many words. Churchill who was kicked out at the end of a war the country had won, largely thanks to him, said that 'a great nation has not only the right, but the duty, to be ungrateful'. Perhaps the British are a great nation.

Is Europe too much of a novelty?

Thatcher, the nanny, has done all she could to change the nation. Everyone agrees on that, even those who could not stand her right from the beginning when she appeared on the doorstep in Downing street quoting St Francis of Assisi.

She has been successful, but there is a lot left to do. A number of Britons are not entirely convinced that the country was going to the dogs in the seventies and feel that the ex-Prime Minister's ruthless remedies were perhaps unnecessary at the end of the day: for sure they hope that John Major's medicine will taste better. At the same time many are convinced (though they are loth to voice their feelings aloud) that by being one of the oldest democracies in the world and having had the largest empire, the British are special – aristocrats. And aristocrats they reckon, always find a way out, one way or another.

They are wrong. Thatcherism has been like a trumpet call blared in the ears of those who were asleep in a sinking ship: hardly surprising that people who have been woken up that way are ungrateful. Pre-Thatcherite Great Britain was not a nation, it was a church in which traditions and institutions such as industry, the trade unions, universities and bureaucracy, were all sacred and perennial. Mrs Thatcher fought this mentality right from the beginning when she became Leader of the Conservative Party on February 11th, 1975, to the very end on November 22nd 1990, when she handed in her resignation to the Queen. Whatever mistakes she made were more a matter of tone and presentation, though occasionally she went too far. The majority of the British people have come to terms with privatisation, but never accepted that some public services should go underfunded. London Underground – too old, too crowded and too dangerous – is a very good example.

On the other hand, the refusal of the harsher side of Thatcherism is no excuse for resuming the bad old ways. The danger is always lurking: the British who hate change are quite capable of doing just that. As a nation they are diehard conservatives: they like their television, their radio, their royal mail and bureaucracy to stay as they are. And rightly so: they are all excellent and should set an example to Europe. But in the same breath they oppose changing even those things that do not work all that well. We could say that the British are arrogant: the idea that they have 'the best in the world' is not dead at all.

As a result the country is full of workers who do their job badly and halfheartedly (as you can read in the *Journal of Industrial Relations* and see for yourself when dealing with a plumber in London). There are still too many old schools churning out large numbers of badly educated pupils – the British themselves say so and the Education Secretary agrees with them. A lot of people from Inverness to Bristol are strill grieving over the loss of the shilling which was done away with in 1970. Even pub landlords find that, though they are allowed to open all day, clients are not taking any advantage of the new opening times, so many have gone back to the old ones.

Old fashioned Conservatives and Labour sympathisers fought side by side against change. The former feared that Thatcherism would force them to change their habits, and felt threatened by the wealth and the values of the nouveaux riches. The latter were terrified at the notion that the working classes would desert ideology for the ownership of a terrace house: which is precisely what happened. Mrs Thatcher's success in the eighties was built on the transfer of Labour votes, especially from the C2 band – craftsmen and skilled workers – to the Tory party, quite a revolution.

Unless Mr Major is as tough as Mrs Thatcher, things could revert to what they were. There is no doubt that the two main parties are tempted to return to a more cosy and comfortable relationship in which they lead the country either together or in turns (a number of Italian Christian Democrats and Communists feel the same way and for the same reasons). The Little Englanders, fearful and isolationist, are ready to come out of hiding and attack. Clothed 1970 style, their heads stuffed with 1940 rhetoric, they know full well that post-Thatcherism is the last chance to put the clock back to the good old times. I met one of them at the end of 1990 in a television debate in Birmingham. When I suggested that the love of tradition in Great Britain was a trifle excessive, my Little Englander stood up and proclaimed loud and clear, 'But the Englishman is God!' so no criticism please.

Such ingrained conservatism could be a blessing if carefully monitored. Any Italian with any sense envies the British love of tradition and respect for institutions. The trouble comes when love of what is ancient and well known turns into fear of what is new and unknown. One gets the impression sometimes that the class system – number one target of the Thatcher revolution – survives because it has always been there. As Martin Amis shrewdly points out in his recent, convoluted novel, *London Fields*: 'Not even a nuclear holocaust can change the class system'. He could be right: not long ago the London High Court in the case of the Duke of Westminister v Lady Porter had to decide whether the working class still existed. It ruled that it was still there, alive and kicking.

The class system survives because everyone seems happy with his lot. The upper classes take pride in their genuine or pretended eccentricities, the middle classes delight in looking at their well mown lawns, and the lower classes sit happily in front of the box watching darts, or staring at the big bosoms on page three. They don't want change. The Italian worker sees a beautiful car and says, 'I'd love to have it', the British worker dismisses it: 'Richman's stuff'. The average Italian is delighted to be asked to an important wedding: afterwards he will talk for weeks on end about it. His British counterpart hates every minute of it and longs to be back where he belongs, with his friends at the pub. In Italy people are apprehensive but they are always on the go, restless and busy, in Great Britain they are quiet and contented: they like things to be as they have always been.

There is no doubt that the British are obsessed with their past: a new museum opens every week. It is a world record but not something to be really proud of: while the rest of the world manufacture goods, they produce tradition. Many have protested against this tendency to turn Great Britian into one huge museum but to no avail. Margaret Thatcher herself met with opposition every time she wanted to introduce anything new. It happened with the pound coin replacing the note, with the new yellow telephone boxes instead of the traditonal red ones, and with the new maroon European passport taking the place of the old stiff blue British one with its little window.

For the same reason Europe is looked askance at: it is new and as we have seen the British people are allergic to novelty. It is quite likely that the former Prime Minister had correctly read the mood of the nation when she stood up loudly against the Currency Union and the 'creeping socialism' of the Brussels bureaucrats. British liberal commentators like to think that it is not so, that the British electorate has always been more European-minded than its leaders. Everyone agrees on the need for a British presence in Europe to prop up France and Italy against German dominance; everyone remembers the 1983 Labour election manifesto with its proposed withdrawal from the EEC. (They dubbed it 'the longest suicide note in history' after labour was flattened at the General Election.) But people prefer to forget that Great Britain has never liked the idea of a united Europe and has not hesitated in the past to intervene militarily to impose its views.

The problem could be that the liberal pundits, and intellectuals, academics and rock musicians with them, may not want to see what they are afraid of, namely Great Britain excluded from Europe and heading the way Portugal is, (it too had a large empire). But the man in the street loves his daily diet of 'Frogs', 'Huns' and 'Spaghetti-eaters'. He does not quite know what to make of the Chunnel but is convinced that the EEC is full of robbers, out there ready to trick the naïve Englishman. When a tabloid came up with the story about lorry loads of British lambs being set on fire by angry French farmers, the whole nation was swept by an anti-French campaign. Opinion polls are there to back all that up: in the Community as a whole, 65 per cent are in favour of relinquishing their national currency for the ECU, and 35 per cent against, in Britain it is the reverse: 65 per cent want to stick to the Pound and 35 per cent opt for the ECU.

Not many people may have joined the demo in Trafalgar Square shouting abuse to the President of the European Commission (Up yours Delors!), but the *Sun* can still boast twelve million readers and one of its editors has been knighted. Even those British who like to think that they are good Europeans firmly believe that at Euro-summits, their leaders are put upon by 'useless, vain glorious, spaghetti-eaters no-hopers' – to quote the *Guardian* (incidentally they mean us, the Italians). A number of educated people, people you would never have thought of, hold the view that the new Europe will spell the end of Old England. We can but hope that they are not in earnest when they get going with the 'Dunkirk spirit' to resist European integration. To be alone against the enemy in the forties was heroic. To be alone among friends in the nineties is frankly ludicrous.

2

Classes

Happily Divided

Take the napkin ring. Forty years ago, according to the *Daily Telegraph*, someone wrote a treatise on it, claiming it was a 'powerful social indicator'. In other words a person's attitude to the napkin ring was the ultimate proof of his social origin, of his place in the 'class system'. The upper classes for example were ignorant of them. Since they had fresh napkins at every meal there was no need to indicate who had wiped their mouth on which cloth. At a village ceremony in the north, when a duke was presented with an exquisite pair of napkin rings he had to be told what they were for, before he could express his thanks. The working classes were unaware of the napkin ring because they used their sleeves instead.

Nowadays all that has changed, especially since *Debrett's Etiquette and Modern Manners*, the upper class's Bible, has condoned the use of paper napkins. But napkins still divide the world in two: the upper classes insist on 'napkin', while the rest call them 'serviettes'. Social climbers say 'napkin', but they think 'serviette': the sort of effort that makes you hopelessly middle-class.

Class, whatever you read or hear, obsesses the British to this day. There have been alterations, but the system remains intact. With Mrs Thatcher at the helm the middle

22

class has mushroomed while the working class has shrunk to the great chagrin of the Labour Party, who have no more masses to mobilise for revolution. The upper class has also been radically transformed: the gentleman is almost extinct. As Philip Mason says in his book, *The English Gentleman*, nowadays they prefer holidays in Majorca to 'the pursuit of moral excellence'.

Any Italian banker, diplomat or journalist living in London and trying to find his way around in English society, will tell you this much: the class system is alive and well and terribly complicated. There is an historical reason for this: since the French Revolution the upper class has been on the defensive and from that position, it has achieved wonders. Until the First World War, it managed to lead a united nation and run an empire with minimal use of force. For that purpose and in order to go on setting an example, the upper classes have always scrupulously avoided any contact with the middle classes. In Victorian and Edwardian Britian, the middle classes were trying desperately to learn the nuances of social behaviour and etiquette. The élite, to remain élite, kept on changing the rules.

What is new today is that the upper classes, worn out by two centuries of pursuit, have let the others catch up. The middle classes, enriched by commerce, have at last learned what to do: they send their sons to Eton, Harrow and Westminster, they stitch four buttons on their jacket sleeves (not two, not three: four). They say 'lavatory' (upper class – 'loo'; working class – horror – 'toilet'). Social mobility has not transformed George Orwell's 'most class ridden nation under the sun', it has simply made the machine more sophisticated. As Italian journalists grow ever more desperate, the British keep on at it.

To this day, the population lives in watertight compartments. Each segment eats, sleeps and lives according to the rules of its own class. The upper classes are fond of old furniture such as leather arm chairs. You will find around their dining room tables, five chairs from four different centuries. If they are going to pieces, so much the better. I recently read in the *Spectator* about the Duchess of Devonshire proudly showing off the holes in her old carpets at Chatsworth. In Oxfordshire, they look down upon the Heseltines since they have found out that all their furniture has been *bought*. Middle-class housewives, on the other hand, are very proud of their designer kitchens and of their dishwashers. These instruments are looked upon with suspicion by the upper classes who perhaps extend to crockery their ideas on personal hygiene. If they ever have one, they hide it and refer to it as a 'washing-up machine'.

Language itself, pronunciation, accent and choice of words, create barriers. George Bernard Shaw, who knew the British well, wrote: 'It is impossible for an Englishman to open his mouth, without making some other Englishman despise him.' There is an abyss between Lady Diana and a Hackney shopkeeper, even when they simple utter, 'Yes, please.' If the shopkeeper tries to pronounce 'actually' like the Princess of Wales, with a sort of sneeze between the 'c' and the 't', her East End friends would be rolling about laughing. Mrs Thatcher, whose father was a grocer and who epitomises upward mobility, was taught to speak like a lady, but she has never learnt the lesson. She lengthens her A's just like the Princess ('salt' becomes 'sorlt'), but then she proceeds to apply the same treatment to O's and 'involve' sounds like 'invorlve'.

Even the authorities recognise the system: the Registrar General has divided the population into five groups according to occupation. Professional people, such as lawyers and doctors, are in class one; class two is made up of semiprofessionals such as farmers, MPs and journalists; and class five includes the unskilled workers such as Underground ticket collectors. But of course the system breaks down when someone like Viscount Linley decides to become a carpenter.

Oxford University recently made a detailed study of the British social structure. The 'Oxford Mobility Survey' contains some interesting results: one in five children of working-class parents will move into the middle class; the middle class has doubled in size since the war. Hugh Montgomery-Massingberd disapproves of these generalisations. In *British Aristocracy*, he warns against the abuse of the term middle-class: 'Nowadays everyone is middle-class with the exception of 900 Peers of the Realm and their close relatives, not many in a nation of sixty million inhabitants.' In his view, British society must be divided into ten compartments: 1) upper-class, 2) lower-upper-class, 3) upper-middle-class, 4) lower-upper-middle-class, 5) middle-class, 6) upper-lower-middle-class, 7) lower-middle-class, 8) lower-lower-middle-class, 9) upper-working-class, 10) lower-working-class. But just as in modern trains, he goes on, these compartments are connected and one is always being pushed about by the crowds going up and down.

Upper Class: Old Wealth, New Poverty

According to Anthony Burgess, the way foreigners perceive Britain is based on crude stereotypes. In a piece called 'On being English', he refers to a regular advert on French television where 'an aristocrat is shown sipping a cup of tea in a dinner jacket, while his house crumbles.' Burgess is right, but so is the unsophisticated French advert. The small landed gentry are gallantly fighting a losing battle against Capital Transfer Tax, vanishing butlers, and ageing roofs. They have been brought up, generation after generation, to withstand the slings and arrows of misfortune, and they can do so in style. In other words, they sip their tea in their dinner jackets while the house crumbles around them.

Let me reassure you, this does not happen to the great nobility. As far as I know, none of the twenty-six dukes is insolvent. Besides, a 1976 Statute has exempted some of the most beautiful houses from some taxes because they are national monuments and the national monuments are inhabited by dukes and not by the lesser aristocracy with its family burden. The cries of pain of this lesser gentry appear every now and again in the letter page of the *Daily Telegraph*, like the nostalgic memories of the landowner in Kent, whose father had eight servants. He had to make do with two Filipinos who had already been in jail eleven times for beating each other up in the basement.

British people like to catalogue their suffering. Someone has even worked out a correlation between the extent of decline and the number of times the telephone rings in a country house, before it gets answered. Gone are the days when the butlers stood poised at the ready: today the average is thirteen rings before you get an answer. Sir Marcus Worsley has a similar problem at Hovingham Hall in Yorkshire where the front door is a hundred yards from the living quarters. 'People go away thinking I am not in, while actually, I am running like a horse.'

Another interesting case is that of Sir Charles Mott-Radclyffe of Barningham Hall in Norfolk, who, unable to stand the idea of clearing up twice, lays two tables for himself every day. Lord Cawdor, who owns 56,000 acres around Inverness, maintains that the disappearance of the 'serving class' has resulted in a deterioration of cooking standards. Before going out to dinner parties, he makes a wager with his wife about the menu: 'Our *bêtes noires* are meat loaves and steaks as tough as crocodile meat.'

In spite of all this, the landed gentry does survive. Let's look at Capital Transfer Tax. In recent years, the small landed gentry has tried all sorts of arrangements in order to keep their country houses in the family. By far the most common practice is to transfer the whole property into the name of a healthy young son. But suppose you get two deaths in the family in the wrong order and the whole estate is in jeopardy.

Local authorities, animal rights activists and heritage

associations can be irritating as well. One foxhunt in five is disrupted by anti-bloodsports campaigners and marquesses and viscounts frequently end up in court. Recently, Lord Hertford had to cough up some £15,000 in costs and fines for having ploughed up a third-century Roman settlement on his property at Alcester. His friend, Lord Montagu of Beaulieu, chairman of English Heritage, turned him in.

The great strength of the upper class which enabled it to foil any revolutions, is its ability to adapt. The small landed gentry, defeated by maintenance costs, has moved into town. They are the *nouveaux pauvres* (they prefer it in French it sounds smarter). Nicholas Monson and Debra Scott, who have examined the phenomenon, describe it as 'running an aristocratic lifestyle on a tradesman's budget', a feat worthy of admiration. The silver spoon ready for auction is their symbol, and their ability to conceal lack of ready cash is legendary. The Thames is their Rubicon: *nouveaux pauvres* all live south of the river. P. G. Wodehouse's Psmith used to say of Clapham: 'I have heard of it, but is its existence really proven?' Battersea is the land of the 'sonlies', which stands for 'It's only five minutes from Sloane Square' (north of the river, of course).

Even the law recognises the divide between the nobility and the lesser aristocracy: the latter have to struggle with the provisions of the various 'Rent Acts', while the former can lease its properties in central London at exorbitant prices. Not long ago the young Duke of Westminster, who owns almost all of Belgravia and Mayfair, appealed to the Court of Human Rights in Strasbourg. He maintained that his human rights were being violated by the statute that compelled him to sell properties to his sitting tenants. He lost the case. But since his assets run to some £2.5 billion, not many tears were shed.

Nowadays, 'upper-class' includes the wealthy bourgeoisie as well, with whom the troubled lesser aristocracy has reached an understanding. In real life this means commercial contacts and marriages. City whiz-kids frequently marry into the aristocracy: he has the cash, she has the name. She will not be driven to tears by his table manners. They both have a public school background, common acquaintances and similar accents. You need a tidy £80,000 a year to run two houses (one in London and one in the country), educate two children, and 'do all the right things.' Small wonder the aristocracy has accepted these crisis measures with such good grace.

Recent statistics and reports on the inner structure of the upper class confirm this evolution. According to the Royal Commission on Income Distribution and Wealth, in 1911 one per cent of the population controlled 60 per cent of the wealth, now it is only 20 per cent. Of the ten richest men in the land, only the Duke of Westminster belongs to the landed aristocracy. The Sainsbury family have made billions of pounds from supermarkets, keeping a safe distance from manufacturing industry. Essex University, in a recent study of the 'very rich', worked out that after the wealthiest top ten, there are about a thousand people with assets over four million pounds and twenty thousand with over one million pounds.

Professor Bill Rubinstein of Deakin University, Australia, has investigated the origin of this wealth for a British television network. He examined bequests that exceeded a million pounds in the 1985 Register of Deaths and came to these conclusions: 42 per cent of the deceased had been born of millionaire fathers, another 29 per cent belonged to wealthy trading or professional families. 'In other words,' he sums up, 'you need money to make money.' Why British television needed an Australian to tell them that, I do not know.

The legions of the middle classes

Sometime ago, an Italian friend of mine made the following discovery during an afternoon shopping trip: in Britain you need four 'thank yous' to buy a bus ticket. The conductor comes up with his machine on his shoulders: he says the first 'thank you' (meaning 'I am here'). The passenger hands over the money with another 'thank you' (I can see you, here is the money). Another 'thank you' from the conductor (read: that is the correct change, the deal is struck, here is your ticket). At this point the passenger takes the ticket and utters an appropriate 'thank you'. You can total up to six 'thank yous' if you do not hand over the correct change. Italians are amused by this ritual; when they have to pay for their tickets at home they normally do it with a grunt. Americans who normally carry out such transactions in dead silence are flabbergasted.

British daily life is full of these harmless ceremonies. They are there not to draw attention to those of us who do not conform to them, but to make daily life more pleasant. If foreigners do not like them, say the British, that is their problem.

The upper and lower classes do occasionally forget. Let's get back on the bus: in a crowd of football hooligans, a few will try to dodge the fare. After an afternoon of gin and tonic, a dignified old gentleman might forget to make his presence known to the conductor. If he is caught out he will pay up, exclaiming, 'I am so sorry.' The vast middle class, about 80 per cent of the population, pays without batting an eyelid, even better, it pays with four 'thank yous'.

The middle class is undoubtedly the strongest and represents Great Britain abroad. There is no class war: the middle classes won it long ago. They possess all the necessary qualities of a victorious army: patriotism, a sense of duty and from 1979 to 1990, a perfect leader in Mrs Thatcher. As we have said before, she decided to adopt middle-class values and to extend them to the whole of the country. The urge to make money is nothing new, but was never really important: the working classes felt it, but could not control it, the upper classes were ashamed of it. In the past ten years, Mrs Thatcher has tried to convince the country that greed is good for you and you should be proud of it. She has been moderately successful: Great Britain is discovering the joys of moonlighting. Some time ago a Minister said, with some alarm on the BBC, that moonlighting represented 8 per cent of the gross national product and that the Treasury was losing out to the tune of five million pounds a year.

Mrs Thatcher used various brilliant approaches to pump new blood into the middle class. Let's look at a few. She encouraged tenants to buy their council houses. Labour was up in arms, not because they did not like the idea per se, but because they thought that their traditional electors' commitment to revolution would weaken if they became home owners. They were right of course; the Tory vote has gone up in line with the increase in home ownership. Today 70 per cent of families are home owners.

Another skilfull move was the invention of 'popular capitalism', a term used by Mrs Thatcher to describe her vision of Britain. The Personal Equity Plan introduces tax breaks for investment in stock up to £2,500. This initiative which has been successful with the less affluent has enraged the Opposition.

Another demonstration of Mrs Thatcher's ability to impose her views came in the late spring of 1988, at the Synod of the Church of Scotland, when the then Prime Minister set out to reconcile her religious beliefs with her policy. She managed to quote St Paul (in his letter to the Thessalonians) and the Old Testament (the Book of Exodus) to prove that wealth creation is profoundly moral. Idleness and the worship of money are sinful, she said, not work and industry. The Scottish middle class, who had been kept in check by its allegiance to the Church, was wooed by the Thatcherite crusade.

Inevitably the top section of the working class would have

overflowed into the middle class, regardless of Margaret Thatcher, but she certainly speeded things up. The old Tory Party with its caring paternalistic image was profoundly shaken. There were only thirty Etonians among the 396 MPs who were elected to Westminster in 1983 with Mrs Thatcher. She was not interested in the social background of her team, but did have a weakness for self-made men. Top jobs in the Government and in the Party went to people like Norman Tebbit and Cecil Parkinson who would rather shoot a fox than hunt it. People like the Marquis of Lothian's heir who is MP for Edinburgh South, and the Earl of Kilmorey, MP for Wiltshire North, prefer prudently to be known as Mr Michael Ancram and Mr Richard Needham respectively.

The middle class is winning everywhere: even the Foreign Office was officially reprimanded for being too plain and 'petit bourgeois' (there must be some truth in this, look at the way British diplomats dress all over the world). The middle class not only preserves Mrs Thatcher's values, but also all the quirks, habits and idiosyncracies which have been a greater tourist attraction than Big Ben and the Queen. The uncontrollable passion of the British for gardening keeps 'Gardener's Question Time' at the top of the hit parade of all four BBC radio channels. This programme, which can be heard on Sunday afternoons, is so popular that gardening clubs must wait for years before being allowed to ask their questions on air. Orpington Argricultural Society, who recently hosted the one thousand six hundred and fortieth programme had filed its request on September 21st 1960.

Other obsessions are: weather forecasts, red buses, black taxi cabs, the countryside, Sunday papers, Sundays spent reading papers, Remembrance Day, red telephone booths and the blue passport with the little window and the royal coat of arms, which the British have long-refused to exchange for the maroon European passport, in spite of supplications from Brussels.

The middle class is so fond of its traditional way of life, that it feels a kind of sympathy with petty criminals, as long as they fit into tradition. Punks, teddy boys, skinheads and especially mods, who are middle-class anyway, are almost accepted as part of life. There is still a fondness for the London fog, even if it doesn't exist any longer. They got rid of it thirty years ago by banning the use of coal in town in the Clean Air Act of 1956; this happened after the great fog of 1952 when 4000 people died. The British know that, but when they come to London they try so hard that they can still see the fog described by Dickens.

The triumphant middle class is very conservative in its habits, it is up to the upper class to introduce new customs. The middle class will follow, but a good deal of time later, feeling its way carefully. One appropriate example is kissing. The average Englishman abroad in international gatherings, suffers nightmares about kissing people socially like the French do. It is a health hazard and a waste of time. For some years now the upper class has accepted this practice: one can often watch prim young ladies at parties stiffly kissing unknown young men on both cheeks. The middle class is still miles away from doing it.

Another characteristic which intrigues foreigners and represents a sort of hallmark of the middle class is their acting talent. Middle-class Britain is where the very great actors come from. George Bernard Shaw said in *Pygmalion* that the British like to hang on to the class system precisely because its rituals appeal to their hidden acting talent. Taking leave at the end of a party is like acting a play, the guest affably proposing, 'You must come round for a drink sometime,' when in reality he does not like anybody around his place. The host, with a broad smile, answers, 'I'll give you a ring,' but he does not mean it. The guest again, 'Do you want my telephone number?', secretly dreading a positive answer. It is up to the host to bring the conversation to an end with another broad smile, 'I am sure you are in the book,' but he knows very well he will never bother to look him up: in any case he has already forgotten the name of the guest.

Another example: on the phone they do not address you with an abrupt 'tell-me' as in Italy. It is, 'How can I help you?' with a high-pitched ending. Guests are warmly welcomed and entertained (often with port and cigars). The goodbyes are enthusiastic: but do not turn up again too soon or you will receive an icy stare. When two colleagues meet, they will part with a solemn, 'We must have lunch sometime.' If you fall for it and enquire, 'Fine, when?', you will get a puzzled look. An Italian might well say: I came, I saw – and I didn't understand a thing.

Where's the fish and chips?

If the working class ever has an anthem, we all know what it will be. I cannot give the music, but here is the complete text: 'Here we go, here we go, here we go (pause). Here we go, here we go, here we go-o (pause). Here we go, here we go, here we go (pause). Here we go-o, here we go.' Readers who are interested in football are acquainted with these sophisticated lyrics; they are the favourite of British fans, who have introduced them in European stadia, together with other less harmless behaviour.

In Great Britain the working classes love football, or more precisely are fond of football, beer, darts, high heels and black suspenders, videogames and holidays in Spain. A sweeping statement possibly, but the British would agree with it, and the working classes will confirm it proudly. That is why the class system has lasted so long. There is a feeling of belonging and complacency in being working-class, as much as in being middle- or upper-class. Each group has its rituals and petty satisfactions and does not envy the other: if the working classes love a pot belly, the middle classes enjoy slaving away in their eight square yard garden, and the upper class delights in its elegance, genuine or not.

Until Mrs Thatcher arrived, this three-tier social structure was reflected in a clear cut political divide: the upper class was Tory, the working class Labour. Since the middle class has always been the largest one, the party capable of securing most votes from the middle class would win the election. Then Mrs T came and set out poaching in Labour territory. This extraordinary feat yielded extraordinary results; Mrs Thatcher won three elections on the trot. An unequalled feat in this century.

The ex-Prime Minister was certainly helped in her forays into the working class by the popular press. Unless you live in Great Britain, it is difficult to grasp the importance of the popular press. Let's look at some figures: the Census Bureau has recently published a report on social trends stating that 11,700,000 people read the *Sun* every day in Britain – it is the bestselling paper amongst the popular press. Thirteen million people read its Sunday sister, the *News of the World*. Both papers were blatantly pro 'Maggie' – the leader, and 'Maggie' was grateful: in amongst breasts and bottoms and advice to the reader (how to spend a million pounds; buy four thousand miles of knicker elastic and stretch it from London to Nicosia and back), one could find regular contributions written and signed by Mrs Thatcher herself and her ministers. It's possible she may have been ashamed of it, but there is no doubt that the advantage outweighed any shame.

The popular press may be coarse, but it is straightforward. In editorials, beginning with 'The *Sun* says', the important sentences are underlined, to make life easier for thick readers. What the *Sun* says is normally hair-raising. In an editorial on Spain not long ago the *Sun* called it 'a country of bloodthirsty butchers.' 'We must not spend our money in that wretched country. Let's leave the Spaniards to their acid wine and their turgid (*sic*) food.' On another occasion, commenting on a speech by the Duke of Edinburgh, the punch line was, 'And now shut up, you silly old ass'.

The recipients of such refined press analysis are called 'yobs' by the British. This is a slang word from the middle of the last century, originally no more than the inversion of 'boy' and with no derogatory meaning. Nowadays it typifies a violent and aggressive youngster, of which there seem to be more and more about. It is the drunken 'yobs' who have caused the English football teams to be excluded from the European Cup. We saw them in action once again during the World Cup in Italy. There are inhibited 'yobs' to whom the 'Club 18–30' proposes parties 'more destructive than the atom bomb'. There are also female 'yobs' with their acrylic attire and bare legs at any time of the year, whose main ambition is to make it, stark naked, to page three of the *Sun*, wearing a jockey hat, with a caption reading, 'Oh, wouldn't we love to be Susie's horse!' Their unchallenged idols are Ian Botham and Samantha Fox, the girl who started off her career, breasts to the fore, in the popular press and can now command a fee of £4000 to open a supermarket.

The trouble with the 'yob-culture' is that it is not always harmless. Faced with a pattern of persistently unacceptable behaviour from hooligans, people have begun to wonder where this urge for physical violence comes from. According to Anthony Burgess, in the old days these violent youths would have been the strength of the army. Now that the empire is no longer there, the 'yobs' let off steam by fighting each other. 'From Agincourt to Port Stanley, history books are full of descriptions of our main talent: have a good fight,' says David Thomas in the *Sunday Telegraph*. It is interesting to note however, that these violent youngsters turn into respectable citizens after the age of thirty. Then they start worrying about the new generation of 'yobs' and what they might do to their teenage daughters.

Luckily for Britain, not all working-class parents rear such children. Up in the north of Britain, in spite of unemployment, some of the lower social strata maintain a dignity inherited from the Industrial Revolution. The miners for example, still have high moral standards which won them admiration during the mad twelve-month strike of 1984–85. Every summer the miners from Wales and Yorkshire migrate with their families to Blackpool. There they dip their children into a tobacco brown sea, spend their evenings under the illuminations and sleep in bed and breakfasts. To the British, Blackpool is a sort of shrine for the working class, and rightly so: it has its own charm and beauty. The 'yobs' prefer to go to Benidorm, where they can get drunk in the sun and learn the language (tequila, senoritas, pesetas).

Like the beaches up north, other traditions of the working class are endangered. You had better hurry if you want to see the last of the workforce that built the empire. The granddaughters of the Liverpool sailors, of the Manchester weavers and Sheffield smelters are deserting, more and more, the Bingo halls which Andy Capp's long-suffering wife, Alice, loved so much. Until recently, the Church and Bingo, and Bingo more than the Church, were their safe havens, the only places where they could go while their husbands were drinking in the pub. Today, only a few dear old ladies still fill their evenings with a glass of shandy and five cards for twenty-five pence. Bingo halls had to survive, so have moved on to video games, cabaret, catering and rollerskating. Alice, who cannot skate, is already fading into the background.

Another British legend, the fish and chip shop, the only place where you could buy lunch for a pound, has suffered the same fate. It all started when they were prevented by law from using newspapers as wrapping. Deprived of the taste of ink, the working class rapidly switched to fast foods, to the great chagrin of some Italians in some parts of England and Scotland who had monoplised the trade. In London there seems to be a fad for greasy fingers: the fish and chips shops are doing well with the smart set.

Two institutions, the pub and the television, are holding

up very well. The British keep on drinking with enthusiasm, spending about £35,000,000 a day on alcohol, more than they spend on clothes, cars and household goods. The average annual consumption per person is about 270 pints of beer, 20 bottles of wine, 9 litres of cider, 10 litres of strong alcohol. This recent statistic includes new-born babies and teetotallers: someone must be going over the top.

One can say just as much for the box. The British man sits in front of it for an average of twenty-six hours and four minutes a week, for women it is over thirty hours. Only three per cent of families own a dish washer, but only 23 per cent have a video recorder. We have no specific statistics for the working class, but we have reason to believe that they are completely hooked on television. The BBC's *EastEnders* and ITV's *Cornation Street*, a sort of homemade *Dallas* and *Dynasty*, have had record audiences. The leading characters, all strictly working-class, have become popular heroes and their adventures, from 'flu to adultery, fill the front pages of the tabloids.

The tabloids and television bear the responsibility for yet another characteristic of the lower class, an extraordinary lack of interest in what happens on the other side of the Channel. It is not xenophobia, because that would require some knowledge of the people you despise. The working class simply ignores foreigners. They are prepared to take an interest in them only when they produce cheaper hi fi systems (Japanese), or drink more beer (Germans), or lose a war (Argentinians), or when you can insult them: when the *Sun* talks about the French it does not write 'French', it writes 'frogs'. Top of the list of dislikes is the European Community, which is accused of being up to all sorts of dirty tricks. Margaret Thatcher understood this very well. She was tough with the EEC, while promising lasting political independence backed by nuclear weapons. The British armies of old marched to her tune.

Do you know 'Punjabi Pop'?

I learned about British ethnic minorities not so much from books or television programmes, but from a woman called Miss Sakina Punjani, an East African Asian, who dresses in a sari and is a newsagent in Holland Park in West London. Like any self-respecting newsagent, she also sells stationery, icecreams, cigarettes, sexy birthday cards, half-price paperbacks, batteries, street maps and disposable nappies. Conveniently, Miss Punjani has opened a Post Office counter in the shop.

What Miss Punjani has in common with the Pakistani owner of Fairway Foods in Kensington is not only their Asian origin, but their working hours. The newsagent in Holland Park is open from six in the morning to nine in the evening. The supermarket in Kensington literally never closes. Some maintain that the owner takes time off secretly in the dead of night when he thinks his customers will not need any frozen hamburgers, Bulgarian wine, toothpicks, deodorant, bulbs or shoe polish.

Faced with such long working hours, the British recoil in horror. But it is convenient to be able to buy two eggs at midnight, so they keep quiet and are full of admiration. Besides, the heroic practices of the Asian shopkeepers are a fascinating mystery: no one seems to know what they do with all the money they make. Their families are here, so it looks unlikely that they would be spending it to go back to Pakistan or India. It is more likely that they intend to buy up Britain, lock, stock and barrel in the not too distant future.

The British are passionately interested in race relations, together with cricket and the Queen. There was a lot of debate in 1981 and 1985 after riots in London, Liverpool, Birmingham and Bristol. The subject surfaced again when the Government decided to introduce entry visas for Indians, Bangladeshis, Ghanaians, Nigerians and Pakistanis.

Before, as Commonwealth citizens, they arrived in Britain and had to convince the immigration authorities of their right to stay. When the Home Office unwisely set a deadline, thousands swamped Terminal 3 at Heathrow, and brought it to a standstill. While Rajiv Gandhi was accusing Great Britain of racism, Labour politicians were making fiery speeches in the Commons and television crews were filming newborn babies asleep in ashtrays in the airports. In the end the Government lost its nerve and had to put everyone up in hotels at vast expense which did nothing for its image.

The publicity such events receive, besides touching a raw imperial nerve, has spread the notion that the 'non-white' population in Britain is numerically large. However, a 1986 survey discovered only 2,400,000 non-whites (some 4 per cent of the population), 40 per cent of whom were born in Britain. According to the 1981 census, many immigrants are concentrated in the capital. In London, five per cent of the population is from Africa and the Caribbean, four per cent from India and Pakistan, and six per cent from other places such as Portugal, Italy, Hong Kong and Cyprus (there are as many Cypriots in London as in Nicosia).

The 'non-whites' are divided up into two groups: the 'blacks' from the West Indies, and the 'Asians' from the Indian subcontinent. Both groups moved to the 'centre of the empire' in the late forties and early sixties, at the time when the Italians were moving from Naples to Turin. They moved for the same reason: industry needed manual workers and got them from anywhere. In Italy it was car factories; in Britain, building sites in London and textile factories in the north.

The majority of the new arrivals did not intend to settle in Great Britain, but they ended up doing so. You can observe the phenomenon in Bradford: 400,000 inhabitants, 90,000 from Pakistan, Bangladesh and India. Unlike the Poles, the Ukranians and the German Jews, who came before them, they have not integrated at all. They still eat, dress and behave, according to their ethnic origins and build mosques (in Bradford there are already thirty). They have four times as many children as the white population, therefore in Bradford one in four pupils is dark-skinned. In nineteen out of seventy-three county schools, seventy per cent of the pupils are not white.

The headmaster of one of these schools was Ray Honeyford, a hirsuite Conservative from Manchester with a working-class background. Mr Honeyford wrote, in an article in an obscure journal, that the ethnic education which was being introduced in the area was a crazy idea. To teach Urdu and allow Muslim girls to swim in pyjamas to protect their modesty, was absurd, 'because the immigrants' decision to become British citizens, implied that they wanted a British education for their children.' If the family wished their children to receive a traditional Indian and Pakistani education, Mr Honeyford went on, they should not expect to get it in the state sector. The school authorities were horrified, the whole town was up in arms and Ray Honeyford was thrown out. In Yorkshire I believe the parents are happy: Pakistani girls still have their swimming lessons in their pyjamas.

When in February 1989, Muslims all over the world were up in arms over the *Satanic Verses* by Salman Rushdie, who is a British citizen, many of the Pakistanis, Indians and Iranians in the United Kingdom had no second thoughts: they sided with Khomeini and their fellow Muslims. In interviews all over Britain they repeatedly confirmed their readiness to carry out the Imam's death threat against the writer. At the 'Italia Cafe' in Bradford, gangs of youths would willing be photographed striking threatening poses, while London corner shop attendants would shake their fists and scream invectives. Most of the media were completely taken aback: we thought that Britain had at least taught what tolerance is, they repeated.

It is difficult to place immigrants in the class system. The Race Relations Acts of 1965 and 1976 try to give minorities equal rights, but give them no place in society. Some people maintain that the 'blacks', some of whom play professional football, and spend their money in the pubs, feel an affinity for the working class. The 'Asians' do not team up with anyone, though the way they like to make money would suggest a de facto alliance with the middle class. A closer look shows that this assumption is correct: until they are rich enough, the Asians float above the class system. When they land, it is straight into the middle class whose values they readily adopt. One of the main characters of *My Beautiful Laundrette* sums it all up beautifully. When accused of being a scrooge, he retorts, 'I am a professional businessman, not a professional Pakistani.'

Minorities will not make it any further than the middle class though. British insitutions are beyond their reach: there has only been one 'non-white' MP since 1987, there are no 'black' judges. In the national press there must be only about a score of 'black' and 'Asian' journalists; the domestic Anglican Church has only one 'black' bishop, the Catholic Church about as many ethnic parish priests, and out of 115,000 policemen only a very few are not white. The Policy Studies Institute conducted a survey based on mock employment applications by British ethnic citizens. The outcome was that it is four times as difficult for a 'black' or an 'Asian' to find work, as it is for a white Englishman. All the figures, whether on unemployment, housing, or violence, paint the same picture: according to a Home Office study on racial harrassment, 'blacks' will suffer thirty-six times as much and 'Asians' fifty times as much as whites. In Southall, Tower Hamlets, Newham, and Waltham Forest, excrement in letter boxes and stones through drawing room windows are a clearer message to any Pakistani family than statistics.

It is in Southall and Newham, where a third of the population is ethnic, that some interesting developments can be seen. Here young Asians, most of whom were born in Britain, seem to be more interested in leading a peaceful,

separate existence than in pursuing integration or working
for the advent of 'British Islam'. Pakistanis do not even try
to be accepted: they leave it to the Italian and French to
ape British culture. They simply mind their own business.
Recently, the Empire, Leicester Square was swamped by
two thousand teenage girls wrapped in their chunnis (a sort
of scarf) and covered in sequins. Escorted by their male
relatives, these young Indians and Pakistanis happily
coughed up ten pounds in order to scream at their local
pop group playing in the West End. If the British take no
notice of them, the Asians take no notice of the British;
sometimes the Asians ethos is very simple. It needs no statement: you just get up and dance to Punjabi Pop.

3

The usual unusual tribes

It is well known that British youths love gangs. As these gangs are born and grow up, newspapers take an interest, parents worry, and youths decide that since newspapers take an interest and parents worry, it is worth while carrying on listening to a particular sort of music and wearing a particular sort of clothing. Therefore many senior citizens now remember the post-war years not by the names of the Prime Ministers, but by the names of the various tribes: 'teddy boys' in the fifties; 'mods' and 'rockers' in the early sixties; 'hippies' and 'skinheads' in the late sixties; fans of the androgynous-looking David Bowie in the early seventies; 'punks' from '77 on; 'new wave' in the early eighties and 'acid house' fans in the late eighties.

In recent years music gangs have declined – only punks are holding on as a tourist attraction – while other kinds have proliferated. Rich young people are doing very well in their undoubtedly eccentric tribes, a term they dislike; the trendy left survives and suffers in silence, pretending not to be trendy and wondering what the hell has happened to the left; the right, a term with no particularly derogative overtone in Great Britain, is blooming. There you will find Margaret Thatcher's eggheads and the City whizz-kids for whom ideology comes second after the payslip and whose main worry is another stock market crash like '87 and '89.

The tribes we are about to visit are all different in wealth, social habits, history and standards of hygiene, but they have one thing in common: their members really mean what they do. Fashions in Great Britain are no pastime: governments are too efficient, the climate is too atrocious and the British themselves too serious: fashions have to become a full-time occupation. In the sixties, at a time when British hippies embraced long hair and filth, their Italian counterparts would discard tunics and sandals and go off to the seaside in Daddy's car. Ten years later came the punks, incredibly stupid but determined: if they protested by cutting their nose with a razor blade, they would do it with a real nose and a real razor blade. Would-be Italian punks came to London and had a fit: in the end they dyed their hair, which is not very painful.

Punks for purists, punks for tourists

One has not heard much about punks lately. In 1977 they created a new social phenomenon by which spitting in the face was elevated to an art form. The critic, Bevis Hellis, wrote in the catalogue of the 'Cynical Seventies' exhibition: 'good art can only originate from bad taste.' If one is to believe him, punks did their bit beautifully, with their attrocious songs and their impossible behaviour. The battered prophets of this strange religion were the Sex Pistols. The British people made their acquaintance on a summer evening in a live television programme in which the four abused a miserable television presenter called Bill Grundy, for a good half hour. They were very young, atrociously dressed, with spiky hair, rotten teeth and weary eyes. Throughout the whole programme they giggled, yawned and picked their noses, pushing their fingers in up to the knuckles. They created such an uproar, that the record firms, whose sales had stagnated since the Beatles, vied to book them. EMI won the race, but were forced almost immediately to cancel the contract because the Sex Pistols were going on undeterred to shout abuse from the stage and insult the Queen. It was bad for the corporate image.

This new movement was christened 'punk', a word meaning something like bad youth. Various people and pressure groups took an interest in it to further their cause. The left saw in it the symbol of the despair of the new generations, deprived of work and hope by the austere measures which the International Monetary Fund had imposed on the Labour Government. The violent right spotted the swastikas on the leather jackets of the new rebels and made advances. The punks took no notice, possibly did not fully understand, and carried on improving their 'mischievous wind-up', the violent stage behaviour which had made them famous. Only once did they play politics, when they boarded the *Queen Elizabeth* and sailed down the Thames in a 'Jubilee cruise' to mock the Queen in 1977. This was not a revolution, more of an insult to the Queen, whom the punks could not stand.

The heroes were the singer and the bass guitarist of the Sex Pistols, Johnny Rotten and Sid Vicious. The former could not sing at all: his music teacher in a recent interview recalled how Johnny Rotten, whose real name was Johnny Lydon, would huddle up in a corner of the classroom during lessons, without uttering a sound. When forced to make a noise he would 'howl'. Sid Vicious on the other hand lived up to his stage name: he stabbed his girl friend, Nancy Spungen, to death. He was sentenced and then released early, and died eventually of a heroin overdose in Greenwich Village in New York.

This unexpected martyr possibly transformed the movement from a passing fad to a deeply rooted cult. Today punks are still around; they meet and celebrate like war veterans. Film director, Alex Cox, has made a film out of Sid's and Nancy's story under the title *Sid & Nancy*. It was a sort of punk *Gone With the Wind*, a statement disputed by the model Debbie Juvenile and the writer John Savage, who were involved in it. On the other hand Jamie Reid, the

Liverpool youth who designed the sleeve for 'God Save the Queen', is a convinced millenarian. He is busy creating an opera with the title *Leaving the Twentieth Century Behind*. When asked whether it would be a musical, a record or a film, he answered 'possibly all three'.

Johnny Rotten's fate is even more interesting. The former singer, so to speak, of the Sex Pistols is now thirty-five, has a German wife who is already a grandmother, and lives on the outskirts of Los Angeles at Marina del Rey, in a castle originally built in the twenties for Mae West. He has changed completely: he got a large compensation deal from his former manager, drives a huge milk-coloured Cadillac and acknowledges that 'to chair two real estate concerns is perhaps a bit much for a former punk'. He cannot stand today's King's Road punks: to his mind they are completely potty and are 'a joke in bad taste'.

They, on the other hand, cannot even imagine that they are despised by their very idol: twelve years on they continue to push safety pins through their nostrils in complete good faith. Punks take advantage of new developments shamelessly: they earn their living by giving in to tourists who run after them with their cameras. In London they are on display as in a zoo in two places: in Trafalgar Square under the statue of Lord Nelson, who certainly would have disapproved of them, and in the King's Road. Every Saturday morning, punk couples sprawl on the pavement waiting for bus loads of Japanese who relentlessly hunt them down as in the old days at the changing of the guard at Buckingham Palace. Their fees are always the same: one pound for a picture, two for filming, five for the take of a mock fight. If tourists do not pay up – Italians will always try not to – the leader growls and flashes the camera lenses with a mirror. At this point everything is clear: either you pay or you run.

All this aggression is, needless to say, just a show. The Punks of the nineties are eccentric but harmless. Every now and again commendable tales about them can be read in the press. There was the punk who decided to switch to another fad and sold all his attire to Somerset County Museum, or the Bournemouth couple who asked to keep a mouse on their heads for the duration of their wedding (the mouse's name was Bulldog, if you want to know). A Farnborough couple went to court when their three-year-old son was expelled from nursery school, because his light blue mop of hair was distracting the other children. A Portsmouth punk sailor contacted his MP when the Navy would not allow him to wear his Mohican hair style in a submarine, due to lack of space.

Strangely enough, it is the Italians, when they come to London, who take up a fashion which has been dead for the past eight years, and they do it very seriously. Some time ago Barone Andrea Belluso di Monteamaro appeared in the *Sun*: this twenty-three-year-old son of a diplomat had learned in London how to use mascara and lipstick and dress up in studded leather outfits a style that had been in vogue amongst the young several years before. I met Cinzia Borromeo personally in the King's Road: she is from Pordenone in north-east Italy, a place renowned for its fiery females. Obviously one still, she strolls about in the snow wearing a minute miniskirt and no stockings. We asked her how was it that she had arrived in Britain ten years late. She coolly answered that to come to London from Pordenone, answering the call of the Sex Pistols, was a perfectly natural thing to do. You must agree this makes sense: if Italians fly to Kenya in search of wild Africa, which is no longer there, and set out for Moscow dreaming of socialism, which was never there, they might as well come to London to keep the tourists happy.

Young Fogeys: Those who choose to be old

Only the Yorkshire moors are more silent in the whole of Britain, than the ranks of the young rich. No signs here of regular trips to Melrose Avenue, the Los Angeles street where young teenage girls think they are adults because they can buy their own cocaine. In the UK the wealthy young disapprove highly of such behaviour: they might buy books about them, but intensely dislike those sorts of cars and that sort of tan.

Rules and regulations, buzz words and habits are totally different. Let's look at the 'yuppies', an American invention of some years ago. On the other side of the Atlantic, they were, and still are, young men and women of some wealth with no children, and very self-indulgent when it comes to cars, clothing and exotic holidays. There have been attempts to introduce this ethos in Britain. Twenty-eight-year-old bachelors with an income of £100,000 a year and a mind to spend it all, must exist here as well. Sure enough, someone wrote a book on the matter and proposed a new British name for them: 'yaps', young aspiring professionals. According to its author, Pearson Phillips, they are all Margaret Thatcher's children, meaning that they have created an élite based on money, merit and appearance and hardly at all on class. Something totally new for Great Britain.

For a few months, these well-off young men got a lot of attention. It was decided that in order to be a proper 'yap' you had to have a German car and Italian clothes for your girl friend; you had to eat expensive 'nouvelle cuisine' in French restaurants, have exclusive credit cards and live in particular areas: Islington, Fulham and Notting Hill. The 'yaps' took over these areas and started renovating houses and streets the previous occupants had happily moved away from. In their wake, like camp followers after the army, came the film studios, the brasseries, the gyms, all run by other 'yaps' busy helping their friends to get rid of their money.

Well, no one talks about these people any longer. Perhaps they were too American, not eccentric enough and possibly not sufficiently rich. Behind this retreating army have appeared new crowds such as the 'young fogeys', literally 'the young old-fashioned people'. Their main characteristics are: they always praise the past, only write with a fountain pen and could stand Mrs Thatcher because she was hyperactive. A young fogey loves architecture in general and neoclassicism in particular: if you never fought the Bauhaus movement or strived to preserve red telephone booths, you do not qualify.

The young fogey phenomenon is recent. The term was coined in May 1984 by Alan Watkins, a political columnist in the *Observer*. In an article meant to provoke the young representatives of a bad tempered and forever dissatisfied right wing, he wrote. 'The young fogey is a libertarian, but not a liberal. He is a Conservative, but has no time for Mrs Thatcher. He is a disciple of Evelyn Waugh and tends to be unsentimentally religious. He hates modern architecture, and fusses about old missals, old grammar books, syntax and punctuation. He moans over the difficulty of buying decent bread and cheddar worthy of the name. He loves to go for walks and to travel by train.' The young fogey's Bible, according to Mr Watkins, is the *Spectator*, whose former editor, Charles Moore, was one of the best examples of this category. The Prince of Wales is 'superfogey', the idol of the brotherhood: he was elevated to this position by popular acclaim, when he bluntly told the members of the Royal Institute of British Architects that their proposed extension of the National Gallery was like a 'carbuncle on the face of an old friend'.

The term 'fogey' was immediately popular, not only with newspapers who took an interest from the beginning, but with the concerned parties. *Country Life* and *The Field*, both magazines meant for the landed gentry and full of pictures of mad looking horses, glorified them immediately, while the traditional press pondered over their political affiliation. They were labelled 'romantic Tories', perfect descendants of Disraeli and Salisbury. In a nutshell, their philosophy advocates the return of 'Merrie England' which the industry and commercialism have methodically destroyed.

Geographically they stop at Dover: what happens beyond Dover does not matter. They do not like the Channel Tunnel presently under construction, not because it is dangerous, but because it is useless.

Faced with this phenomenon, British publishers did not waste time. Immediately it was possible to buy *The Young Fogey Handbook* by Susan Lawrey and *The New Georgian* by Alexandra Artley and John Martin Robinson. Both books are full of long lists. All the things a young fogey does not like. For example: the present, the sixties, television, computers, electric or electronic typewriters, modern architecture, the EEC and sociologists, not merely because they can be confused with social workers. Or all the things a young fogey adores, such as a reputation for being learned, witty, austere, and a trifle intolerant. He also loves ancestors, house parties, hunting and women, both beautiful and clever, and money, especially belonging to the above-mentioned ladies.

Their appearance is also worth noting. Young fogeys show a profound liking for dressing unfashionably and to that end they use a lot of time and energy, though they are loath to admitting it. Shirts must have vast, floppy, droopy collars; suits even when brand new must appear worn-out (a great fogey, the writer and critic A. N. Wilson, maintains that clothes must only be changed when they stink); ties must be creased; for the ideal haircut, viz the leading characters in *Chariots of fire*; useful extras are braces and waistcoats and trouser clips for cycling, an activity of which the young fogeys are apparently very fond; no beard, of course: possibly a small Anthony Eden moustache, and even that is a bit risky.

Now you might wonder where the female young fogeys are and how they dress. Well they do not exist. Fogeyism is an exclusively male club. Of course there are beautiful, wealthy, well educated young ladies who share their values, obsessions and beds and take part in the rituals, as wives, sisters or colleagues. Some of them, who converted from feminism to family life, are held in high esteem. Outmoded Italian names like Arabella (already a Sloane favourite), Griselda and Ortensia might even enthuse a young fogey. The problem is this: young fogeys have not made up their minds about sex, whether it is a blessing or a nightmare; but they know this much: in 'Merrie England' women used to keep quiet. They might as well go on doing so.

A house for the 'New Georgians'

The term 'New Georgians' stems from the period between 1714 and 1830 in which four Hanoverian kings ruled, each of them called George. At that time architecture was unadorned, furniture elegant and hygiene nowhere to be found. Nowadays a number of young Britons, not many but true eccentrics, have decided that that time was somehow quintessentially English and want to salvage whatever they can. The operation has turned into an obsession. In their belief that Victorian architecture is uninteresting and modern stuff a true disaster the 'New Georgians', normally very well educated young men, buy up crumbling properties in the worst parts of London and live there with their families. True to their label of 'creative preservers', they want to preserve, protect and salvage everything and they are able at a glance to date a chimney pot or the leg of a chair. The motto is 'The Greens can have nature, we take care of the rest'. Because of their strict adherence to their beliefs, and we shall see later on what this means when it comes to toilets, they are much admired, but they have few followers. There may be plenty of old houses in Italy, but I fancy very few would seek to emulate them.

We shall start from the house, which is the overwhelming passion of the 'New Georgians'. If you have been to London, Dublin or Edinburgh, you know this sort of building:

the front is rather flat, with the brickwork showing. The windows are all the same, symmetrical. A few steps lead up to the doors which are decorated with a fanlight. The houses are normally terraced. The sight of an eighteenth-century terrace is like an aphrodisiac to the 'New Georgian'. He is so obsessed by this sort of building that he will move anywhere for the sake of living in it. (In this he is different from other young, well educated men who are prepared to put up with the misery of a basement as long as it is in Chelsea or in Kensington.) Bloomsbury, the most elegant Georgian district, is financially beyond most people, therefore 'New Georgians' have ended up in far less exciting parts of London such as Clerkenwell, Hackney, and Spitalfields. This last is an extraordinary place: squashed between Liverpool Street Station, Petticoat Lane and the first East End factories, it consists of very few streets. That is where the extremists live and that is where you must go if you want to understand them. Spitalfields, a place as dismal as Hogarth's engravings, is a monument to British eccentricity. The 'New Georgians' decided to settle there about twelve years ago, after ninety out of two hundred and thirty buildings had been bulldozed and nine more were under threat. A group organised a sit-in and set up the 'Spitalfields Trust', collected money to restore two houses and sold them. Since then eighty per cent of the buildings have been rescued. Some time ago an estate agent put up a house for sale in Wilkes street, a genuine example of Georgian architecture, with no water or electricity, for £225,000. It could be worth £425,000 after renovation. Seven or eight years ago it could have been bought for £40,000.

The extravagances of the 'New Georgians' are particularly interesting because in their folly, they bulldoze their way through problems. If you cannot install heating for the sake of the wall panelling, it goes under the floor; the chairman of the Spitalfields Trust has transformed a hollow bronze statue into a radiator. For the sake of authenticity (their pet obsession) some 'New Georgians' will only use candle light (most of them, though, found a compromise in the form of a 25 watt bulb acceptable).

A cottage industry has sprung up around these people: there is an architect who specialises in bathrooms and who is an expert on bricks and their colour (bright red up to 1730, burnt siena afterwards, and yellowish in London after 1800). Another expert studies fragments of original wallpaint under the microscope in order to match it. The most fanatical of all is probably Dennis Severs, a thirty-nine-year-old Californian, who lives in a 1724 house in Folgate Street: five floors, nineteen rooms, 120 candles, and straw for the horses outside the entrance. He also organises guided tours, which suggests that while he may be a fanatic, he is certainly not stupid.

The genuine 'New Georgians' live in these uncomfortable houses amid scarce furniture and a lot of chaos (the French call it *désordre Britannique*). From the outside, exotic food smells waft in: the 'New Georgians' share Spitalfields with a well established Indian community to whom art is no deterrent from curry. Inside there are less mysterious odours. Neil Burton, an architect who specialises in this period, maintains that the original Georgian lifestyle was rather smelly: people believed then that hot baths would give you migraine and cause impotence. The 'New Georgians' – who are British after all – have had no difficulty in rapidly adapting to this lifestyle.

These are the pursuits, but the phenomenon has also touched other sections of society. Estate agents have jumped on the band wagon and have hunted down these properties all over London. If you want to buy one now, not only do you need the cash, but you must be prepared to suffer: as is often the case, a few Georgian terraced houses are buried in council estates. A good example is Cassland Road in Hackney in the East End where a basement – two rooms plus bathroom and kitchen – has been sold for £60,000. If you cannot afford the original, you can buy copies: look at Grafton Square in Clapham, south of the Thames. And if you cannot afford the copy, you can rent, from £3,250 a week or less, in Dorset Square (NW1).

If you can neither afford the original, nor the copy nor the rent, you might have to resort to theft in order to bestow a Georgian look on your house. According to the police there has been a spate of thefts of original items: doors disappear (market value: £500), chimney pots (£50), metal bath tubs (£200) and most of all fireplaces (up to £25,000 for an original Adam fireplace). In 41 Upper Grosvenor street, the banister and all the doors vanished during the night. Not far away three chaps pretending to be working for the Town Council, actually removed old slabs from the street (market value, £20 per square metre). Apparently, in their defence, they quoted Henry James. 'Of the present we can only see the profile, it is the past we can look face on.'

A style for the Left

Amongst all the moaning which goes on in the British left after electoral defeats, when they want to show that they may not have many votes but at least they have a heart, the drabbies make an amusing noise. They are young socialists who like being shabby and pursue a mystical, glorifying poverty. In a country which rightly or wrongly considers itself as the hothouse of new trends, their case is taken very seriously.

Ideally the drabbies are children of the sixties. They are green, pacifists and feminists: hardly ever extremists but always indignant. They always have a profession, but it must not pay too well. They drive third-hand cars and the way they dress suggests that they must assemble their clothing in the morning with their eyes shut. The state of their clothes suggests also that they might have jumped on it before dressing. They are the true 'anti-yuppies' with hobbies such as

Indian music, politics and macrobiotics, and they are proud of it.

A section of the Labour Party backs them and their vision of 'grassroots socialism'. Against them are all the faddies who fill up London night clubs, write in journals they produce for their own needs and how to fulfill them and are behind all the harmless fashions we will eventually ape in France and Italy. They hold one single grudge against the drabbies, though they halfheartedly accept them as socialists: they are a relic of the sixties, and in the sixties socialism lost its style. Look at Woodstock: it was an orgy, all those sweaty bodies: decidedly bad taste.

Michael Foot is the great drab guru. He used to project quite a reasonable image with his velvet jackets, checked shirts and woollen ties. In 1983 he challenged Mrs Thatcher in the General Election sporting an Albert Einstein hairstyle. He was flattened. Today his crushing defeat is attributed to his choice of image. Peter York, in his book *Modern Times*, maintains that 'the Warrior Queen (Mrs Thatcher) projected on to the nation her style exuding strength and purpose, while Michael Foot dragged on in his worn out jackets, pretending to be an ordinary person. But ordinary people had no use for an ordinary Prime Minister.' Peter York, whose *Sloane Ranger's Handbook* is well known, adds that only the executives with their silly smiles on plane ads have a worse image than the drabbies.

The campaign against the 'drabbies' and for a 'new style in socialism' throws up new prophets all the time. One of the noisiest was Robert Elms, who was writing for *The Face*, the style magazine which is a must for all Italian girls as soon as they arrive in Britain (they may not understand any English, but they can always look at the pictures). Elms, the self-styled 'most elegant man in London', is convinced of the need for a crusade against the shabbiness of the left. In an article in *New Socialism* under the title. 'Style wars: let's ditch the Drabbies', he argued that 'style and left used to be synonymous, and style came from our very roots. It is time we go back to them.' He proceeded to recall how 'in its international history, socialism has always been aware of the power of style. From the stark simplicity of the red flag to the Sunday best miners used to wear to go out to dance; from the revolutionary propaganda of the Russian activists to the designer chic of the Italian Eurocommunists. But in England the pacifist look has taken over and the comrades with their turtle neck jumpers want to convince us that style is a dirty word.'

On this particular point, i.e. the style of the good socialist, there is a regular quarrel between two London weeklies, *City Limits* and *Time Out*. The former is the drabbies' Bible: they love its black and white, rough paper and unadorned graphics, the latter is the yuppies' darling. According to *City Limits*, *Time Out* is no longer the voice of the radical left in London: it is taking a stand against progressive movements. *Time Out* is enraged by these accusations. According to its publisher, Tony Elliot, the magazine is firmly on the left, but does not believe in shabbiness and in wooing all the grumblers of the capital.

Battles of a similar nature, only noisier if possible, are waged on the rock music scene. The Style Council and Red Wedge have for some time been drumming up support for the Labour Party among young people. While Red Wedge wholeheartedly supports Neil Kinnock, the Style Council champions the 'elegant left'. The singer Paul Weller, in spite of a few strange initiatives like when he turned the 'B' side of his record into a party manifesto, is an intelligent person with a degree and reasonable appearance. He had managed to find a space for the left on the pop scene, next to Boy George and Wham! when a new rock group appeared claiming to represent the real left, more interested in class struggle than fashion. They are the Redskins whose songs bear titles such as 'Kick over the statues', 'The Power is yours' 'Keep on Keeping on'. Only the drabbies, and not even all of them, buy their records, but the Redskins are undeterred.

The tribulations of the left 'looking for a style' are endless. When you are not in Government, you have a lot of leisure; Labour are using this spare time to improve their image, like other socialist parties in Europe. But they are miles behind in spite of their determination. They now have a new slogan, 'We put people first', a new colour (not red but grey) and a new manifesto 'Freedom and Fairness', the sort of stuff likely to depress Bolsheviks. They even thought of banning the singing of the 'Red Flag' at the end of the party congress in favour of something more modern. If they opt for Rod Stewart's 'Sailing', the drabbies will go into mourning.

Turn right for the Revolution

First we will privatise the nuclear industry, legalise incest and prostitution, and advocate castration for rapists. Then we shall move on to abolishing income tax, social security, and the National Health Service. We shall privatise all public services, including the police and prisons. And finally, barring any revolution, we will legalise euthanasia and we will abolish civil marriage, 'a pagan and disrespectful institution'. All these ideas and many more were incorporated in the manifesto of the Federation of Conservative Students, the home of the noisy 'New Right' which has prospered in the eighties. These 'Conservative students' who haunt Tory Party conferences handing out literature, were a pain in the neck for Mrs Thatcher, reminding her constantly of an old adage: you must control fanatics, or their zeal may become embarrassing.

Ever since its 1979 General Election victory, the Conservative Party and its youth organisations have been waging a war of attrition. Absolutely overwhelmed with enthusiasm for the new Prime Minister, immediately nicknamed 'The Warrior Queen', the Federation of Conservative Students silenced the more moderate young Conservatives and moved towards the extreme right. They are at loggerheads with the Tory establishment who cannot stand them: they have even called for the expulsion of Edward Heath, too wet for them, and as for John Biffen, former Party Whip and for a short while a possible challenger to Mrs Thatcher, 'he must be locked in a cage hanging from the ceiling in the Commons'.

Mrs Thatcher could not in any way be pleased with the Conservative students. One prominent member I'm told chose to spend his holidays armed with a Kalashnikov in the company of the Nicaraguan Contras, and the Federation also circulated 'I love South Africa' badges. At the 1985 conference they chanted 'Thatcher, Reagan, Botha, Pinochet!'; obviously the ex-Prime Minister would rather have been with Ronald Reagan in different company. Afterwards, they damaged premises at Loughborough University, paid up and promised never to return.

Fortunately there are other more presentable groups in the 'New Right', but even they can give the traditional Tories a fit. The latter favour dialogue with organisations such as the Institute for Policy Studies, the leftish think tank set up in 1988 and whose director is Baroness Blackstone. Let's look at the Policy Unit, a unique, fascinating institution, staffed by people in their twenties who busied themselves helping Margaret Thatcher to put the nation back on to its feet.

The Policy Unit worked in close conjunction with the ex-Prime Minister, just above her on the second floor of 10 Downing Street. Altogether there were eight people: two from Trinity College, Cambridge, the others either brilliant civil servants on secondment or graduates poached from the private sector (Shell, Rothschild Bank, British Leyland, etc). Their task was to advise Mrs Thatcher on economic and social questions, assuming that she was ever prepared to listen. In the early seventies there had been Lord

Rothschild's think tank (the Central Policy Review Staff); in 1983 it became the Policy Unit. The director was Brian Griffith, an economist with a chair at City University. It was he who worked out 'Christian and moral justification of the production of wealth', a theory which Mrs Thatcher adopted with enthusiasm. These young eggheads, who cycled to Downing street, were very young and very clever. One of them, Christopher Monckton, who is invariably seen with waistcoat, bowler hat and rolled up umbrella, is better known as the 'walking anachronism'. One of his pet projects was the abolition of any controls on rents in the private sector. Interviewed over his hobbies by *Who's Who*, the heir to Viscount Monckton of Brenchley answered: 'Nihil humanum a me alienum puto.' It is not surprising that when *The Face* encouraged him to 'join his contemporaries and go and eat a pizza', he paid no attention to the suggestion.

This is the fresh blood of the 'New Right' which was behind Margaret Thatcher's crusades: privatisations, pension scheme reforms and curbing unemployment. They all know each other and they all help one other. Take the five friends from Trinity College, Cambridge, for instance: two were in the Policy Unit, two were personal advisers to junior ministers and the fifth, Charles Moore, edited the *Spectator*, the weekly Bible of the intellectual right. The oldest must be thirty-five now.

There are other dens of the 'New Right': Lord North Street in Westminster, for example, headquarters of the *Salisbury Review*. This is one of those journals the intellectuals are forever mentioning and never buying. Professor Roger Scruton is behind it: in his early forties, he is considered the most innovative philosopher of the new batch of 'British philosophers'. He professes a number of original ideas. To his mind 'the country must first be rid of coarse intellectuals, of wets and of loony leftists', after which 'the Government of the nation will be handed back to the messy, incompetent or shamefully inactive politicians.' Then Professor Scruton and his intellectual friends will be able to 'return to their desks to read, write and listen to good music'. Contrary to expectations, he does not seem to want to reach a wide audience; as he cheerfully acknowledges, the *Salisbury Review* is the journal with the lowest circulation in the country, a thousand copies sold every three months, 'but this does not matter at least as long as everybody believes we are important'. Besides Professor Scruton can always taunt his opponents from his column in *The Times*, where he was critical of Nelson Mandela himself. He reserves his more profound considerations for the *Salisbury Review*. For example: 'Thatcherism will sweep clean the New Corruption, the rot of self-perpetuating privileges in the maze of the Welfare State', or 'socialism is a temptation of the human mind: it is wrong, but it must be dealt with'.

We cannot for lack of space visit other holy places of the 'New Right'. There is the well-known Centre for Policy Studies, the breeding ground of Thatcherism, which Sir Keith Joseph set up in 1974. The present director, the affable thirty-year-old Oxonian David Willets, likes to use football metaphors to make his point: 'Our scope is to push on to the right, to create enough space in the centre, to allow Ministers to score.' There is also the Institute for European Defence and Strategic Studies, an offspring of the American Heritage Foundation, which under David Frost's chairmanship, 'intends to promote western values in international affairs'. And of course there is the Adam Smith Institute which would even privatise royalty, if it were possible; at the moment it is busy examining the success of small enterprises, and the misdeeds of 'the small clubs which control British public life'. We will end with the Coalition for Peace through Security, whose objective is to expose communist propaganda. The claim to fame of one of its senior members, apparently, is to have infiltrated a militant section of the Labour Party, to move it to more moderate positions; he managed a hasty retreat before his colleagues found out the truth and poked his eyes out on the spot.

4

London, the adventures of a capital

In order to understand the radical transformation of this city, it may be helpful to look at Notting Hill. Italians know this part of London very well. Every Saturday morning, especially when it is raining, they arrive at Portobello Road street market eager to buy junk for its weight in gold. Londoners know the place as well: it sums up the development of the capital. In the middle of the last century, Notting Hill was inhabited exclusively by the wealthy bourgeoisie: its white frontages and communal gardens, close to the centre, not far from Hyde Park, made the ideal residence in town, more elegant than Chelsea and more affordable than Belgravia. During the Second World War, the houses, which had already become expensive to run, were taken over to accommodate the homeless. After the war the rich did not come back; the Caribbean immigrants decided that the place was central and cheap and settled there. That's where they rioted in the scorching summer of 1958.

The only whites who had the guts to stay on were those who could not afford to go anywhere else: poor fellows, artists and intellectuals, who eventually attracted other poor fellows, artists and intellectuals; these in turn enticed liberal well off youths, who were followed by plain well off youths from the City and by lawyers with their families, thrilled to live in a borough other than South Kensington. Ten years ago a first floor flat, three rooms, bathroom and kitchen, was £15,000, today the price is £200,000. The Caribbean immigrants are fleeing, some of them with bulging pockets.

This phenomenon is called gentrification; it has happened in Islington in the north and is currently happening in Clapham in the south. The most admired achievement at London cocktail parties is the purchase of a house prior to gentrification and consequent steep price rises. Naturally the British seem to be better than foreigners at that game: French diplomats and Italian bankers know they will stay in London only three years; they would rather not experiment and end up opting for well established districts. Therefore mews houses in Belgravia and Kensington basements are full of young foreign couples who swear they like it there, while in Victorian houses at Clapham Common – south of the river, miles from anywhere – live English families who today put up with a regular tube journey an hour long, in the hope of making a packet tomorrow.

The property price rises, which have only recently stopped, have been mind-boggling. For some years it has been a steady twenty per cent. That has been reflected in rents: £500 a week for a flat in a fashionable district (Belgravia, Knightsbridge, Chelsea, Kensington and Holland Park) is not unheard of. The nation was recently stunned by the realisation that two rooms in central London were as expensive as a castle in Scotland, inclusive of grounds. The 123-year lease of a one-bedroom flat (living room, bedroom, small kitchen and small bathroom) in Chelsea was put on the market for £155,000. At the same time Monboddo castle in Kincardineshire was offered for the same price. Robert Burns not only found inspiration in that sixteenth-century building, but could lose his way in the eight bedrooms, four halls, various bathrooms and five-acre grounds.

The increase in property prices has had some strange consequences. The hunting down of graveyards, of which there are as many as 103 in London, is a good example. Greedy property developers are after these plots, where English people bury their dead and stay on for a friendly chat afterwards, as the Italian poet Foscolo pointed out. The

Borough of Westminster learned it at its own expense: it had sold off three cemeteries (Mill Hill and East Finchley in North London, Hanwell in Ealing) to a property concern, for a token price of 15p in order to save £300,000 a year maintenance costs. The grounds were then sold to another concern appropriately named Cemetery Assets Ltd and eventually to a Swiss group. When the three cemeteries appeared again on the market, they were being offered for £2 million as 'long-term property investment' (the owners hoped that the local authorities might eventually grant planning permission). There was a general uproar: the relatives of the dead asked whether their loved ones were part of the deal, Westminster City Council ratepayers were not satisfied with 15p and enquired after the £1,999,999.85 balance.

The rising cost of living in London has other less gloomy consequences. The population, for instance, is decreasing: in 1970 it was almost eleven million people for Greater London, now it has stagnated at nine million and a half. Managers will not move to the capital, not even for a promotion. Firms on the other hand are very generous with their 'London weighting', which applies to people living in Dover, Oxford or Southampton as well. The price hikes on the property market encouraged sitting tenants to buy their council houses just as the Government had encouraged them to. Inevitably that practice created a rift in the working classes. If you had a job, you could have a mortgage and buy your home, if you were both poor and unemployed, you were out in the street. The Tory Government is not too keen to spend public money in subsidised housing. Many families have ended up at public expense, in appalling bed and breakfasts in Bayswater and Camden: parents and children all in one room, and shared washing facilities. If bed and breakfast landlords are all too pleased with the money they are making, the local authorities are not: Camden Borough almost went bankrupt after it totted up £23.5 million in hotel bills.

The situation in suburbia is very different and more

serene. In Richmond; actors, bankers and retired professors pretend not to see the airplanes landing on their heads and interfering with the television reception, as long as they can live on the edge of the park where Henry VIII used to hunt deer. Putney is for those who cannot afford Richmond; Wimbledon is for those who cannot afford Putney. Ealing is where the BBC crews go when they want to film the British petit bourgeois in action. The houses are all the same: bow windows, roses in the garden, patterned settees and patterned wall to wall carpeting to hide the marks of frequent TV suppers. That part of town which tourists persist in ignoring has not altered in sixty years. The critic Cyril Connolly wrote some years ago, that 'if slums make good breeding grounds for crime, middle-class suburbs are hothouses of apathy and insanity'. Obviously he had never been in Naples or Palermo.

Londoners passionately love the borough in which they live and are devoted to it. It is unusual to hear 'I am a Londoner', but the statement 'I live in London', followed by the name of the borough, is commonplace. If you say 'I live in Hampstead', you want to make it known that you belong to the wealthy bourgeoisie, if you admit a Battersea address, south of the river, it means that you would have liked to live in Chelsea, but you could not afford it. Even in Streatham in south-east London, people are proud of their borough, while in Hammersmith, to the west, on the way to Heathrow, you will be told of the pleasures of Sunday lunch by the river, of Coleridge who lived there and of the West End, so close thanks to public transport.

Public transport is both an obsession for the whole population and something they can quite legitimately be proud of. Londoners adore their Underground in spite of the 1987 King's Cross tragedy in which thirty people died because of the strange idea of hanging on to old wooden escalators in a maze of tunnels. They know that it is the oldest (1863) and the longest (over 400 km) in the world, and love the eccentric names of some of its stations: Seven Sisters, The Angel, Elephant and Castle and so on. There are 250 stations in all (from Acton Town to Woodside Park) along nine lines. Everyone is acquainted with the twisted drawing of the Underground map, something a nervous child with lots of felt tips could have done. It dates back to 1933 and purposely ignores distances and topography for the sake of clarity: it has not changed much since. The London Underground, 'tube' for the English and 'subway' for the Americans, ferries 700 million passengers every year (not many compared with Paris, New York or Moscow). Some stations have been renovated in bad taste: Bond Street has chairs and parasols, Baker Street souvenirs of Sherlock Holmes, Tottenham Court Road colourful mosaics, possibly to cheer you up when you have been mugged. The cleanest lines are the most recent: the Victoria Line, completed in 1971 and the Jubilee Line, completed in 1979. The Piccadilly Line, linking the centre to Heathrow, is the most efficient: some mischievously say it is to impress foreigners, while the Labour Party maintains that the Government intends to privatise even the Underground, and keeps some of it in good shape to entice customers. The most smelly, inefficient and dangerous is the Northern Line (black on the map) which cuts across the town from north to south and seems to attract attempted suicides (about fifty each year). Regulars call it the 'misery line' and like to describe its failings while travelling: 'My goodness!, the stink at Elephant and Castle was particularly atrocious this morning; at Euston the platform was so crowded; at Kennington the waiting time longer and more mysterious than usual.'

Anything concerning the Underground fascinates Londoners. Indignant editorials appeared in the press over the misadventures of two buskers by the name of Extremely Frank Jerry and Bongo Mike, Jeremy Halm and Mike Kay in real life, who moved from playing in the corridors to entertaining passengers in the trains. When arrested, they kicked up an enormous fuss, denouncing the police constable who had confronted them. Playing in the Underground is no offence, they maintained: passengers do not have to pay anything and have never complained. We, they went on, are professional players of 'situation music, i.e. music which matches various circumstances'. Not surprisingly their hit, 'This train is bound for Heathrow' turns into 'This train is bound for Cockfosters' as soon as the train reaches the airport.

But not even the Underground, in spite of its size, can solve all the transport problems in London. Some parts of the town, such as the section of the East End next to the river, are extremely badly served by public transport. Something has been done: the Docklands Light Railway now connects the 'new town' built where the port of London once was. You can fly to Brussels and Paris from the City Airport (only a small plane, a Dash 7, is suitable for the runway and there are noise pollution problems). Sometime ago some crafty entrepreneurs realised that in London there was also a river and thought of organising an express service by boat. Soon a hydrofoil should link Chelsea and Greenwich: the voyage should last 30 minutes, with seven stops.

The idea of using the Thames, which cuts across the town from west to east, had already been considered in the last century. It was discarded after a series of accidents involving steam-powered vessels on the Thames caused more deaths than colonial wars: between May 1835 and November 1838 there were twelve collisions and seventy-two fatalities. In 1847 the *Cricket* blew up (thirty dead), in 1878 the *Princess Alice* sank (seven hundred dead). One hundred and eleven years later, in 1989, it is the same story again with the *Marchioness* pleasure boat. Fifty-seven people who had gone on board for a party perished. Today there is no public service yet, but there are private riverbuses: the *Daily Telegraph*, for example, operates a ferry service between Westminster and the Isle of Dogs to encourage journalists to move from Fleet Street to the Docklands. On winter mornings you can watch them board and disappear in the mist like dead souls on the Styx.

The constant deterioration of road traffic has convinced Londoners that the time has come to make use of the river. Lately, as you can read in many surveys and reports, the number of cars converging on the capital is constantly increasing and traffic jams have become terrible – by British not Italian standards – while there is an epidemic of unauthorised parking. The corner stone of all the traffic in London, according to the Metropolitan Police, is Hyde Park Corner. If traffic comes to a standstill there, Park Lane and Marble Arch will follow in a matter of minutes, Bayswater and Edgware Road will soon clog up, and the paralysis will rapidly spread to Victoria, Westminster and along the Thames embankment. Some time ago someone worked out how quickly this 'mega jam' would spread from the centre to the suburbs: seven kilometres an hour, faster than a car at rush hour.

A few naïvely hoped that the building of the M25 ring road, which took fourteen years and £125 million to build, and is 192 kilometres long, would be the answer to all the problems, but it was not to be so. As soon as it was open, the M25 was clogged with traffic in daytime, and at night became the playground of the Porsche fanatics engaged in setting records for a round trip on it (to date, 68 minutes). That, it has been noticed, is a sign of the times: in the old days motorists, when driving on a new motorway, would have slowed to admire the flower beds on the central reserve.

For a passionate view on London traffic problems, ask the taxi drivers. Just half a question, and they are off. The cabbies hate cyclists because they are small and wriggly, buses because they are big and bulky. They do not like motorbike messengers either, 'criminals', that's what they are, nor minicabs (unfair competition); as for Heathrow airport management, levying a flat fifty pence rate, that's daylight robbery. But above all they hate pedestrians. A cynical old cabbie explained his theory in a television programme. 'When pedestrians do not cross on zebra crossings, they are calling your bluff, if you let them pass, all two hundred of them will cross in front of you, foreigners looking in the wrong direction.'

There are fourteen thousand black cabs in London, almost all oldfashioned FX 4: the new Metrocab, which looks like a hearse, is not very popular. The taxi drivers number eighteen thousand, some sharing a car; it is a very closed profession, reminiscent of freemasonry in its strange rituals. Training is called the 'knowledge' and consists in learning by heart all the streets in London; the 'butter boy' is the new one who just passed his test; 'I have been legalised' stands for 'I did not get my 10 per cent tip'. Thirty years ago one in seven was of Jewish origin, now there are some women and ethnic minorities among them. Tariffs are reasonable: about £4 to cross the West End. Londoners get about satisfactorily by taxi and public transport: there has not yet been any official proposal to bar private traffic from the centre. In fact the lack of parking and the crowds of traffic wardens deter anyone from driving into the West End in daytime.

Londoners venture to drive into the centre only in the evening. Sleepless German film makers, pennyless French artists and Italian businessmen without their wives have, over the years, realised that London closes down at the time when Paris is getting excited and Berlin gets going. Pubs and cinemas, public transport timetables and sadistic restaurant proprietors, all conspire to send Londoners home and foreigners to their hotels just past eleven o'clock. Of course there are exceptions: night clubs where young royals behave like uncivilised peasants and uncivilised peasants dress like royalty; saunas and dim Chinese takeaways; sadomasochistic dens where you are only allowed in if you wear studded leather outfits.

If night life is either nonexistent or steamy, evening life

is very bubbly if that is at all possible in spite of it being civilised and lukewarm by nature. Theatres are doing well on the whole: annual attendance figures have gone up by one million compared with 1982 and a number of shows are always sold out (*Me and My Girl*, *Les Liaisons Dangereuses*, *Starlight Express*, *Cats*, *Les Misérables*, *The Phantom of the Opera* and the most recent, *Miss Saigon*). A closer look, however, shows that the situation is not as brilliant as all that. For a start almost all the successful productions are musicals, and almost all of them are the work of just one man, Andrew Lloyd Webber. A large part of the audience is made up of first-timers, inexperienced theatregoers brought up on a diet of television, and tourists. The number of Americans has increased by 70 per cent in the past four years. On the occasion of one of the very last performances by the original cast of *The Phantom of the Opera*, tickets changed hands for up to £1,000.

Traditional theatre is having a rough time. Plays in the West End are often forced to close down after a few performances. Some companies are doing particularly badly: the Royal Shakespeare Company has had disastrous seasons at the Barbican and has accumulated enormous debts. The director of the Old Vic first put some obscure names such as Ostrovsky, Lenz and N. F. Simpson on the bills, then complained that tourists' philistine tastes and their insane passion for musicals were turning London into a cultural desert; possibly an excessive statement. 'Never trust theatre managers,' George Bernard Shaw used to say. The best plays usually make it to the West End from the fringe: this was the case for *Serious Money*, a play which heartily castigated the City and its inhabitants and struck a chord with the many British who cannot stand them either.

It is a good time for cinemas as well, which is rather surprising considering that 50 per cent of Londoners own a video recorder and like to play with it at home. Attendance figures in cinemas have doubled since 1984. At that time the British were complaining that their own national film industry was going bust; now that is doing well, they still complain: the films are too depressing they say. The debate followed the criticism by the Oxford historian, Norman Stone, against the latest British releases, which were accused of giving a distorted, mad vision of the country. The films in question were: *The Last of England, Sammie and Rosie Get Laid, My Beautiful Laundrette, The Empire State* and *Business as Usual*. The story usually took place in grotty suburbia, with a lot of sex (preferably homosexual), bad language, violence and extreme poverty thrown in. Derek Jarman's *The Last of England* doesn't even have a story: it is a collection of apocalyptic images of London with gangs of desperadoes roaming the Thames embankments. The public was divided: for some young liberals, Margaret Thatcher's Britain was almost like that and they welcomed something other than *Gandhi* and *A Passage to India*, in the British film industry. The Conservatives were disgusted and asked for subsidies to these new directors to be cut.

Apart from going to the cinema, what you do in London in the evening depends on your age. Classical music is very popular with the over twenty-fives with an educated taste and a solid bank account. There is a lot on offer at the Barbican, the Royal Festival Hall and the Royal Albert Hall, to mention but a few: it is hardly ever a problem to get tickets even for the most prestigious performers. Some time ago, when the pianist Arturo Benedetti Michelangeli gave a recital, an Italian lady booked two tickets over the 'phone on the very morning of the day before the performance. She cried when she rang up her friends in Milan to tell them the good news.

Eating out is even more popular than the theatres, cinemas and concerts. Londoners have always loved it, and they go on doing so in spite of the rising prices. Dinner for two in an ethnic restaurant is about £15 (normally an Indian place called 'Standard' or 'Star of India' out in suburbia), £20 for a Greek meal around Tottenham Court Road (retsina and a waiter ominously ready with his guitar), £25

(Chinese restaurant in Soho or Bayswater), £35 (Italian restaurant with spaghetti drowning in the sauce: if you complain they tell you that is the way the British like it), £100 at Suntory, the Japanese restaurant in St James's, which was recently castigated by the *Good Food Guide* for a twenty-one per cent hike after the award of a Michelin star. The really tricky ones are the Anglo-French restaurants in grand hotels (Anglo describes the food and French is just an excuse for an outrageous bill).

The younger generation who prefer to drink a lot rather than eat badly, give these places a wide berth. The young trendies usually go to night clubs and to make life difficult for outsiders, they have invented 'one-nighters', places which are 'in' only on one specific night of the week. The foreigner freshly arrived must find out where to go and when to go there. For the Hioppodrome in Charing Cross Road, Thursday is the night (Monday for homosexuals and their supporters); all through the week the place is full of au pairs on their evening off and of winners of package tours to London. The Mud Club which has been 'in' since 1981 is packed on Fridays. You must go to the Taboo on Thursdays if you can get past the Australian disguised as a soft-boiled egg (no misprint: soft-boiled egg). The Wag Club in Wardour Street where actors and rock stars go, has been the most popular club on Friday nights for the past three years. Its latest buzz word, 'The Seventies are back', was immediately followed by the appearance of lots of bell-bottomed trousers on the London Streets, to the great delight of *The Face*, *Time Out* and *i-D*, always on the look out for new fads. Acid House parties appeared at the end of 1988. In a nutshell they consist of crowds of madmen dancing to some obsessive music organised by a disc-jockey (hence the term 'house music'). The standard dress is tee shirts with the drawing of a smile on, head bands and various other psychedelic optionals, sixties style. Acid House fans are said to use an hallucinogenic substance (acid) called Extasy; that alerted Scotland Yard and induced the BBC to

ban the use of the word 'acid' from all broadcasts including
Top of the Pops.

I cannot help touching briefly on prostitution while talking of London night life. If one is to believe regulars, the
capital is disappointing and not just because the fear of AIDS
has developed a 'look but don't touch' syndrome in even
the most willing sinners. Legislation and repeated raids have
turned Soho from the red light district of old into a place
almost suitable for family outings at any time of the day or
night. There are some clubs geared to foreign businessmen
and their credit cards, such as the well known Gaslight at St
James's, and there are still the girls from Liverpool around
Paddington. 'Escort agencies' have even found a place in
literature: Paul Theroux's novel, *Dr Slaughter*, was a great
success and so was Michael Caine's screen adaptation called
Half Moon Street. And finally there are the stickers with
which prostitutes will go on advertising in telephone booths,
promising 'merciless whipping' and a 'good spanking by the
headmistress' to whoever will visit them. The telephone
comes in handy because in Great Britain it is an offence
to accost a prostitute in the street; the spanking from the
headmistress enlightens you on British sexual tastes.
Foreigners who are not informed well enough, but still want
to misbehave, will wander all night aimlessly.

The standard Italian tourist, who would explain London to
the British given a chance, but is reduced to doing so four
times over to his wife, has experienced some slight difficulties lately. For example, some customs which he did not
understand and, perhaps for that reason, had come to love
have been changed. Pubs can open all day. The Home Secretary said it was a matter of common sense. The old hours
of 11 am to 3 pm and 5.30 pm to 11 pm were introduced
during the First World War so that munition factory
workers would not come to work half drunk. The First
World War has been over for a long time now, so the law
has been altered. The Minister disregarded a detail: tourists

choose to spend their holidays in a country where it rains
all the time in order to enjoy the quirks of the British way
of life. If you pass sensible laws, you take away the quirks
and you are left with the rain.

There are other surprises. The October 1987 gale
changed the appearance of London parks. Someone took
the trouble to count the casualties of that night when the
wind blew at 100 miles an hour: 300 trees in Hyde Park,
285 in St James's Park, 17 in Green Park, 350 in Regent's
Park and 700 in Richmond Park. All in all, 3,000 were lost
in London and another 2,000 had to be pulled down for
safety. At Kew Gardens it looked as if a giant with an axe
had been at work all night. Eighty per cent of the trees at
Syon Park came down. The Italian tourist may not be as
knowledgeable as the average Londoner who mourned for
weeks his *Davidia Involucratas* and *Ailanthus Altissimas*, but
he can certainly appreciate a disaster when he sees one.

Other visitors' obsessions were radically altered years ago,
but they have not noticed yet: Carnaby Street, the symbol
of the 'swinging London' of the sixties, for instance. You
can waste your breath explaining to your Italian friends that
it is a place English people would not think of visiting;
nevertheless they go there with their cameras and preconceived ideas and bump into other tourists under an archway
saying, 'Welcome to Carnaby Street, the most famous street
in the world'. Crafty Parkistani traders, crouching behind
mountains of 'University of London' tee shirts, greedily
watch out for new arrivals. We tried, to no avail, to convince
some very well-informed visitors that the only attraction of
Carnaby Street was that it had unwittingly become a sort of
museum of all the fads which have besotted British youth
in the past twenty years. There are lots of raincoats and
jackets left over from the mods (1962) in the shops; next to
these are flower power Indian tunics (1968), skinhead vests
with the Union Jack on (1973), punks' studded collars (1977)
and finally the skimpy black jackets favoured by the new
wave (1980). The only interesting thing in Carnaby Street

at present, is Mary Quant's emporium: the ageing mother of the miniskirt believes that the street will eventually become fashionable again. If that were to happen, Italian tourists would be vindicated.

To confuse the tourist further, other high spots are undergoing radical transformation. The Albert Memorial, for instance, is about to collapse. Queen Victoria had it built in memory of her late husband: now the iron structure is badly corroded, and a recent technical report talks of imminent collapse (whether it will really be a great loss, is open to debate). Piccadilly Circus has been spring cleaned: renovation works have taken a good eight years and have caused Eros to be moved several times. The mascot was originally a Victorian monument to the seventh Earl of Salisbury (why a philanthropist should be represented by a small, plump, naked boy is not very clear). Harrods as well, is about to be changed from top to bottom. Italians normally experience some difficulty in prouncing this name, but love to show it off on the green-coloured plastic bags in the arrival lounges back home. The present owner, the Egyptian, Mohamed al Fayed, decided to invest £25 million to restore it to its original Edwardian style. The project is in the hands of an army of interior decorators who have at their disposal old photographs and documents. The renovations, started in 1987, will take five years and affect twenty-five acres of halls and corridors.

When not busy getting lost in Harrods, Italian tourists like to be in the open air. On Saturday mornings there are so many of them in Portobello Road, that you can no longer make your comments in broad Italian without being overheard, which is rather a pity as this is one of the attractions of a holiday abroad (incidentally, Caledonian market on Friday mornings and Camden Lock on Sundays are safer). Italians are also exceedingly fond of musicals, the brilliant British invention which attracts into the theatre even those who do not understand any English. For some mysterious reason *Starlight Express* has been a great hit: what it boils down to, is just a dozen madmen skating around in circles and unfortunately never falling down. Visits to nineteenth century buildings, such as the House of Commons, are always extremely popular: tourists will persist in believing that they are mediaeval – obviously Gothic revival sells well. I am leaving out on purpose some embarrassing pastimes Italians like to indulge in when in London, such as an evening out at the Talk of the Town in Covent Garden. This is where innocent tourists in the hands of unscrupulous travel organisers end up spending the evening with over-weight dancers, conjurors and their rabbits. This London will never change, not in the nineties, not in the year 2000. At best, if Italians still fall for it, they will be able to attend the 'Party of the Millenium' with slimmer dancers and more rabbits.

5

Going North

From the Channel to the Hebrides, by Austin Rover

One might well start an end-of-summer journey from Brighton. The town is typically British, right in the south and depressing enough to inspire an urge to leave it quickly. Even Graham Greene did not like it: when he wrote *Brighton Rock* in 1938, he recreated the town from top to bottom, a contrast with Mexico and Indochina which he described so realistically. Day trippers are the curse of Brighton. They come from London in the morning – it's fifty-five minutes by train – and go back before dark. They spend the day hanging around the promenade, visiting the Pavilion – a kitsch monstrosity built by George VI when he was Prince of Wales – and gulping down a microwaved hamburger before they go away. The real tourists, the elderly gentlemen in tweed jackets and hats, the sort who can be seen driving their Austin Cambridges at a steady 15 mph, peer down at them from the verandas and venture out only when they know for sure that they have gone.

Leaving Brighton and the south coast behind, we aim north on the A26. We are trying to look as British as possible: a right-hand drive silver Austin Rover Montego, the *Ordnance Survey Road Atlas* and the *AA Illustrated Guide to Britain*, which like the cushion in Italian cars, is almost always present in British ones, even though it is seldom used.

The road crosses the hilly East Sussex countryside not far from Glyndebourne, where every summer rich people from all over Europe and a small number of opera lovers gather for a picnic among the sheep. We plan to bypass London to the East on the new M25 ring road and to cross the Thames via the Dartford Tunnel. The river divides two worlds: in the south, Sussex and Kent are rich and green; at Tunbridge Wells it would be easier to find an elk than a Labour voter. The town was very well known in the eighteenth century for its thermal springs, until someone discovered that breathing sea air was socially and physiologically acceptable. The smart set moved to the coast and Tunbridge Wells became Royal Tunbridge Wells to make up for it. North of the river, we drive through the fringe of the East End. This is where the real tatooed Londoners, who love beer and big busts, live. Eastenders love to migrate to the Essex and Suffolk coasts on summer weekends. The smart set, who picnic at Glynebourne and go to Ascot, would not be seen dead in these places. They do not like the noise of the stereos and the smell of chips, have no desire to come nose to nose with their half naked plumber and could not care less for striptease biros which reveal a topless girl when turned upside down. We of course thought that these were very good reasons for going there.

Clacton-on-Sea, on the Essex coast, is a typical example. In the sixties the mods and rockers, the former with scooters and raincoats, the latter with leather jackets and motorbikes, used to come here to riot at Easter and on bank holidays. Today, visitors are more subdued: working-class Londoners cart their brave children to the beach to look for worms in the sand in the rain; in town fathers go to pubs, mothers to Bingo. The Bingo caller does not read out the numbers, he chants: 'two and two, twenty twoooo'; four and three, forty-three . . .' The women look bored as they check the numbers. They are all plump, with stiletto heels and bright red toenails. All around are the prizes looking on menacingly: huge soft toys which have not been seen in Italian fun fairs for ages.

Clacton-on-Sea also offers other attractions. The most visible is the pier with its amusement arcade: at the very end a restaurant serves bacon and eggs, and cheese and pickles at any time of day. The cheese is always cheddar and after one of those dark-coloured pickles you long for a beer. But of course, there is no beer at the restaurant, you must go to the pub, and the pubs are on the promenade. At the entrance to the pier a middle-aged band blare out rock music through their loud speakers. The drummer is out of breath and the base guitarist looks like Tom Jones. The OAPs take it all very seriously and tap rhythmically: that is British popular music.

From Clacton, thanks to the Austin Rover and in spite of the Ordnance Survey Maps, we arrive at Walton-on-the-Naze, a depressing holiday resort where the BBC recently filmed a documentary on the rituals of British seaside holidays in the fifties: adults dozed, children played, teenagers were bored. Today is the village fête: all the nearby villages have prepared floats on which three girls aged five, twelve and about twenty sit surrounded by flowers and salute the crowds: they are the queens. The twenty-year-old looks bored to death, but people do not seem to realise. At 2 pm the pubs are doing good business – parents drinking, children waiting outside.

A few miles north of Walton, over the Stour estuary, is Suffolk. In the old days the county had the reputation for being the laziest in the kingdom. 'Please don't rush me, I'm from Suffolk,' can still be seen on some old bumper stickers. There is even a village called Great Snoring. Today Suffolk, like the rest of East Anglia, is very rich: there are small businesses everywhere. Felixstowe is the fifth largest container port in the world and Lowestoft, the easternmost town in Great Britain, has a big fishing fleet. Great Yarmouth, another high spot of British tourism, is also an important port. We go to the Marine View: from the window we cannot see the sea, but to make up for it, the room is decorated with flock paper. According to the visitors' book, there have been no foreigners here for ages. The owner, however, swears that he had a South African customer at the beginning of the summer.

There is an immense beach at Great Yarmouth, with windbreakers to provide shelter from the wind which blows straight from Scandinavia; there are tidy gardens and a promenade full of neon lights, noise and couples strolling arm in arm. There are also plenty of wet weather entertainments and plenty of wet weather as well, here and along the whole coast. (Mrs Eileen George, aged seventy-two, from Brixton, says that this year, besides Great Yarmouth, she went on a package holiday to Margate, Brighton, Eastbourne and Southend, and it rained everywhere.) There is a homemade version of Madame Tussaud's, where if you look closely you can tell the difference between members of the Royal Family and characters from *Dallas*, a haunted castle and several fun fairs with bizarre names: it only costs ten pence a go for a trip on the flying saucer. The real problem with the place is the sea itself: it does not meet the minimum EEC standards. Children do not seem to worry though: as soon as the sun appears, they dive into the grey-coloured waves.

On Sunday morning we leave Great Yarmouth and head inland, towards the Norfolk Broads – thirty or so shallow lakes set in green surroundings and linked by canals and rivers. The Broads are man-made: the original inhabitants made them by digging out peat, which in turn encouraged flooding. Nowadays tourists sail on the Broads at weekends. As a Norwich couple told us while enjoying the sun and the white wine at the stern of their rented vessel: 'You could sail, but it is safer to use the engine to avoid bumping into other people.'

In the westernmost part of Norfolk, the flat countryside crisscrossed by canals is just like Lombardy, the main town is King's Lynn, Lynn to the locals. Today this attractive small town on the edge of the Wash, with its buildings with evocative names, like Hanseatic House or Greenland Fishery House, has a Dutch, contented look, like the rest of East Anglia. Further north you cross the line from the Wash to the Bristol Channel which divides the wealthy south from the poor north. Actually, Lincolnshire does not look poor at all: probably its strong agricultural economy has saved it from all the problems which beset Yorkshire or Lancashire and their heavy industries.

Grantham is the first town on the A1. For millions of people this name means only one thing: Margaret Thatcher. She was born here on 13 October 1925 above her father's corner shop. Her father, Alfred Roberts, was a grocer and local councillor, mayor, magistrate and founder member of the local Rotary club as well. Some years ago, his house was turned into a restaurant, The Premier, specialising in Victorian cooking. Whether because the East Midlands had no use for Victorian delicacies, or because of its very name, the place went bust. Now the shop is up for sale for £180,000. The Pakistani newsagent who told us all that, is certainly not going to buy it: her ghost – he says – could be roaming the place.

His Grace, the tenth Duke of Rutland, like any motorway fastfood proprietor, sells snacks to visitors. The only difference is that we are in Belvoir Castle in Leicestershire. The British, for unknown reasons, write 'Belvoir' and say 'Beaver'. The duke who lives in a wing of the castle and does not consort with the plebs, is not for sale. Almost all the rest is: £2 to go in, £1 extra for a guided tour and just over £4 for two plastic swords. On the way out, in front of the souvenir shop, you are invited to 'trace your ancestors' (£3) because '96 per cent of surnames are related to a titled family.' I duly paid £3, and I am still waiting to see where the Severgninis fit in Leicestershire.

The visit to the castle, exclusive of food, cost £7. One

hundred thousand visitors come in every year, that's £700,000, more than enough to pay for the upkeep of the building and the gardens. Add to that other sources of income, such as mediaeval tournaments and tourist attractions and you can see why Margaret Thatcher would have been proud of His enterprising Grace. I tried to check my arithmetic with a member of staff, an old gentleman in a tweed jacket, but I did not get very much out of him, he seemed suspicious of a nutty foreigner who was talking money instead of asking about the fifth Duke who plotted against Queen Elizabeth I and ended up in the Tower of London.

Driving north from Belvoir, you enter Sherwood Forest where Robin Hood lived happily making life difficult for the clergy, the rich, and the Sheriff of Nottingham. People still talk around here of the man who could split a willow wand with an arrow four hundred paces away and many places bear his name. Both Barndale Forest in Yorkshire and Sherwood Forest claim to be his birth place. In Yorkshire they say that they can prove that a 'Robyn Hode', the son of a woodman, was born in Wakefield in 1285 and that he took part in the Duke of Lancashire's revolt against King Edward II in 1322. In Sherwood country they treat this as a pack of lies and to prove that Robin Hood is one of them, they have dotted the countryside with his statues. Tourists come, see what little is left of the forest, spend their money and the local council is satisfied.

Between Nottingham and York are the South Yorkshire coal mines and some of the most impressive graveyards of the industrial Revolution: Sheffield, where the steelworks died; Bradford where the textile industry has come to an end, and Leeds where the manufacturing and clothing industries are no longer. York's main attraction is the Minster, something not even the Japanese or the Koreans managed to copy: every year, 2,500,000 people come to see it. More than any other town in the north, York has managed to withstand the crisis of the British manufacturing industry which resulted in the loss of 2,000,000 jobs between 1979 and 1981, for the simple reason that Rowntrees (manufacturers of 'After Eight') are in York and British Leyland is in Birmingham. All over the world, people eat British chocolates, but buy German cars.

Through North Yorkshire, a land of cyclists and impossible dialect, you reach the 'North-East'; that's Durham, Tyne and Wear, and Northumberland. This region has a collection of unenviable records: the most crimes, the most deaths from cancer, and the most unemployed, apart from Northern Ireland. The natives are called 'Geordies', have a comic accent and use words of Scandinavian origin. According to Austin Mitchell, the local Labour MP, there is more drunken vomit per square yard here than in the rest of Britain, and 'wife beating' is still a popular sport. AIDS on the other hand, is almost unknown: I have been told by a friend of mine, who is local, that 'in the North-East homosexuals are for beating up, not going to bed with.' Notwithstanding all this, he goes on, people here are generous and like to support lost causes. Possibly this is where the last of the working class culture still is.

The capital of this odd paradise is Newcastle, which has 285,000 inhabitants. We arrive in the pouring rain. In spite of the perennial mist on the car windows (are Austin Montegos built like that on purpose, so the British can feel at home anywhere?), we can see clearly that for some mysterious reason this is an attractive place. We cross the Tyne to get to the town: the iron bridges look like outsized Meccano toys. In the centre, perverse town planners have allowed the building of a huge windowless shopping centre. In nearby Gateshead, opposite the Scotswood council estate, there is another shopping centre, the 'Metrocentre': obviously northerners like them. It is the largest in the EEC, as they are sure to tell you. Why you should have the largest shopping centre in the EEC in one of the most depressed regions of the EEC is a question open to debate. For Margaret Thatcher it was enough to have it there: when she was charged with neglecting the north of Britain and not repaying the debts of the Industrial Revolution, the 'Metrocentre' was invariably her answer. The trade unions maintain that the shopping centre is doing well because people have no hope for the future: they would rather spend now than save and invest. The extreme left say it is all poppycock: people are there to look around, not to buy.

We meet Peter Carr, director of the 'City Action Team', another quango which should get the economy moving. Mr Carr, a friendly fifty-year-old with an ex-army look, is in charge of liaising with the Departments of Industry, Employment and the Environment, which is in charge of Local Authorities. He is adamant: the 'Metrocentre' is a great success. It was built in record time on the worst site in Newcastle, a former steel dump, using only local workers and materials. Mr Carr has confidence in the future of the region: 'We must convince people here that the days when yards employed fifty thousand people are over, jobs must be found elsewhere. Obviously it would be marvellous if factories moved up here from the south where costs are 30 per cent less than in the London area.' Luckily, he goes on, the Japanese have arrived and they have chosen the North-East as their bridge-head into Europe. Nissan employs two thousand people near Sunderland and Kumatsu, the second largest mechanical diggers manufacturer in the world, has settled at Birtley. The Geordies to start with were a bit traumatised by the Japanese work ethic and practices, but money is money and they gave in pretty soon: now they all regularly do Japanese gymnastics in their breaks.

We also questioned Martin Eastel on the future of Newcastle. He is the Director of the Northern Development Board, which has been set up jointly by the trade unions, employers and the local authorities. Mr Eastel, a man of about forty with a sense of humour, comes from London; he dresses like a Londoner, but is perfectly happy where he is. 'Here,' he says, 'I can live better, I can afford a bigger house and better leisure activities.' The one hundred and fifty associations aiming at stimulating job creation, perplex him: as long as the businessmen in the south are uneasy about the north and the Government increases interest rates as soon as it smells inflation, the north will not get out of the swamp. 'We must not rely on the landed gentry: they would rather look out of their castle windows on an undeveloped, quiet landscape, than on to a factory. The civil servants whom the Government sends up here to get the economy going, come from the old colonies: they mean well but they don't have enough funds,' moans Mr Eastel, while we have lunch in a brasserie totally decorated in pink and deserted. With its French name it looks like a space-ship, landed by mistake in Newcastle-upon-Tyne.

If any Scotsman realised that an Italian in an Austin Montego has just arrived in an attempt to discover and describe Great Britain, and in particular one that has been shaped by Mrs Thatcher, he would not be pleased. For a start, the term 'Great Britain' does not really apply up here. It was just about bearable when the empire was being built, but now with nothing really left to share, the Scots and the English prefer to ignore each other. In this part of the world, Margaret Thatcher was about as popular as a hole in the head, as any Scotsman would be only too pleased to tell you. In the 1987 General Election, out of seventy-two seats, the Conservatives, defending twenty-one, lost eleven and two Scottish Office ministers were defeated. From that day the ex-Prime Minister took to visiting Scotland to try and improve her prospects. The Scots admired her determination and pretended to listen to her.

We arrive in Scotland from Newcastle by the longer route: first west up to Carlisle and along Hadrian's Wall, which is still visible here and there to the great delight of the local Tourist Office, and then north, into the region which in mediaeval times was called 'Galwyddel', the Gaelic for 'the land of the strange Gaelic Celts', and since 1974,

Dumfries and Galloway. Don't be fooled by the romantic landscape, that is where the most stubborn Scots live. In medieval times they fought English domination; in the seventeenth century they signed the 'Solemn League and Covenant', in which they swore to allow wind to whistle through their bones, rather than accept the bishops appointed by the King of England; and in the eighteenth century, after the Unification Treaty, the Levellers opposed land reform and used to pull down dividing walls at night time.

We follow the valley of the Tweed up to Lothian. In the capital, Edinburgh, the annual, chaotic arts festival is under way – a good reason for carrying on towards Stirling, the heart of the 'silicon Glen', so named after the three hundred electronic industries from all over the world which have settled there. Seventy of them are American and apparently very pleased with the location. The *Washington Post* said some time ago that engineers transferred from the States, loved to report back home how they were late to work because they had been stuck behind a flock of sheep. A little further to the north and you are in picture postcard Scotland. The A84 climbs up to Fort William at the foot of Ben Nevis, the highest mountain in the United Kingdom with its crowds of exhausted mountaineers. Forty-six miles further, on a narrow lane, is Mallaig. Here we smell the ocean: it is time to stop.

Mallaig is first and foremost a port and survives on fish and tourists. The local population understandably respects the former more than the latter, because they produce an income all the year round. Tourists, on the other hand, only come in the summer and spend a few hours waiting for the ferry to Skye. The local vicar, who runs a bed and breakfast place and leaves his slippers behind on the night table, says that the fishing boats look for herring and hake hundreds of miles out in the Atlantic, well beyond Rockall, and stay at sea several days running. In the harbour, the owner of a deepfreeze warehouse intrigued by the foreigner who wants to know the difference between whiting and haddock, talks of the cold but snowless winters. There is also a lot of wind and in the evening people at the Royal National Mission to Deep Sea Fishermen sit around formica tables and watch the television. At the O'Clamhan pub in the High Street, local youths drink beer and take no notice of tourists who stick out a mile with their tartan ties. A folk group sings 'Over the sea to Skye'. We can see the island beyond the Sound of Sleat, so off we go.

The first thing we notice on our arrival on Skye, is that everyone is called MacDonald or MacLeod – the two clans which have dominated the island since time immemorial with occasional bloody fights – and that the place is full of odd legends about elves, fairies and magic banners to spread on your double bed if you want lots of children. Another local celebrity is Bonnie Prince Charlie, the Young Pretender, who landed in Scotland in 1745 with seven men and then moved on to fight George II with a whole army of Highlanders. He was defeated at Culloden and fled to Skye dressed up as a woman. Today pubs, restaurants, sandwiches and newborn babies are all named after him.

Apart from that, the local population is cheerful and harmless enough. In the summer, tourists come because of the landscape: a lot of heather on the hills, tall dark mountains and castles. The opening to the public of MacLeod Castle at Dunvegan is regarded as a brilliant operation, not least by the owner who pockets £2 for each visitor and lives in Aberdeen. On Skye, the unemployment rate is 21 per cent, but in the capital, Portree, they tell me it is a big joke: the locals queue up for the dole and then look for odd jobs. In the warmer season they mind sheep or go out fishing; in the winter they become masons, plumbers and carpenters for the local hotels and bed and breakfasts. The owner of one of them, Mrs MacLeod, obviously, tries to convince us that on the island there is also a night life, apart from the fairies and elves. In her drawing room, next to the electric log fire, there is a collection of books on the Royal Family.

She maintains that Prince Charles is very elegant in his kilt and she will not accept that his ears stick out.

From the northernmost port of Uig, the Caledonian Mac-Brayne ferry service links Skye to the Outer Hebrides. The crossing takes three hours during which the natives are at the bar. We arrived at Tarbert, the one and only village on Harris. The name of the place means 'narrow land between two bays across which boats can be pulled': it seems the locals have been doing just that to while away the time. On Harris, in fact, there are only sheep, white sandy beaches, icy blue sea, terrible mosquitoes with a taste for insect repellent and more sheep. The population talks Gaelic, observes the sabbath, and tries not to crash into one another when driving on the only road around the island. There is only one lane with places to allow cars to pass. Normally that is where the sheep are.

In the middle of the seventies, Andrew and Alison Johnson moved to this strange paradise. Both Oxford graduates, they abandoned jobs, friends and relatives, bought Scarista House, the old vicarage overlooking the bay and turned it into a hotel. Alison is short with curly dark hair and looks more like someone from Calabria in the south of Italy, than an Oxford intellectual, in spite of her woolly jumper. She has written a book about her experiences, entitled, *A House on the Shore*, which sold well in Britain. It became the bible for people who dreamt of drastic solutions to their problems after a squabble with their bosses. In the wake of the book, Alice Johnson has acquired followers and the hotel more clients. 'They come here and gaze at me,' she says. 'Luckily, when Autumn comes, the weather chases them away: north winds, south winds and west winds that can blow a car off the road, and rain every day.'

North of Harris is the island of Lewis. The place is flat and bare; the main town is Stornoway, where Harris Tweed is made. The town has two celebrated public conveniences, in great demand on Friday nights after closing time. They are called the 'Old Opera House' and the 'New Opera

House', because people come in with a bottle in hand and stay on for a song. In spite of its small size, there is even a newspaper in Stornoway: the *Stornoway Gazette*, which appears on Thursdays. Main topics can either be Mr Dave Roberts and the new breed of bats he has just discovered (seven columns and a picture of the bat), or the possibility that the Outer Hebrides might become a nuclear dump (three columns). From Stornoway, under the watchful eye of a family of seals, the Caledonian MacBrayne ferries sail up to Ullapool, a Scottish port founded by the British Fishing Federation in 1788. The village recently celebrated its bicentenary and sells tee shirts to the tourists with 'We have been fishing for the last two hundred years' written on them. From Ullapool, the A835 crosses the Highlands to Inverness: here Loch Ness ends and the fun begins.

First, let me tell you that in the autumn of 1987 a crowd of American and British scientists conducted a three-day sonar scan of Loch Ness, codenamed 'Deep Scan', which did not produce the monster, but predictably infuriated the locals. The reason is not difficult to understand: if American sonars did not come up with anything, it meant that about a third of the population around Loch Ness – some four thousand people, each of whom swears to have seen the monster – was insane. On the other hand, if the scientific instruments had proved beyond doubt that Nessie was an overweight seal or a huge carp, it would have been a disaster for the tourist industry: no one would come all the way here in the hope of seeing a fish.

With all this in mind, the locals quietly did all they could to sabotage the operation. First, they produced only twenty-four motor boats, not forty as originally promised. That way the boats could never cover the whole length of the lake at any one time: if Nessie could not be found, obviously she had dodged them. Scotsmen in full kilt and tartan caps, attended all the press conferences and protested noisily over suggestions that the monster was an invention of the local tourist office. The meetings were due to take place each evening at six o'clock in the Clansmen Hotel. That was a bad idea: the Scots used to get there an hour early and when the press conference started, one hour late, they were completely drunk and ready to disrupt it with disapproving noises.

Luckily, everything turned out for the best. Lowrance Electronics sonars showed three strong 'mid water contacts' (at 80 metres, 170 metres and finally, quite clearly at 180 metres). Each time the contacts only lasted a few seconds, showing that the object, whatever it was, was moving. A similar study carried out in 1982 with less sophisticated equipment produced similar results. Opinions on the matter are very varied: according to the organiser of the expedition, the shaggy, natural scientist Adrian Shine, it is an enormous predator fish at the very top of the food chain (in other words, it is a fish so big that it eats everybody else). The Lowrance Electronics experts respectfully pointed out that you need a fish of an incredible size to produce such clear signals at that depth, and anyway why should it go that deep where there is no food. The chairman, Mr Darren Lawrance, said that the scientific results made him think of a 'very large shark'. That outraged the monster's fans. Sween MacDonald the 'clairvoyant of the Highlands', predicted that the next expedition would prove the existence of a family of plesiosauruses at the bottom of the lake: it would not be the first time that animals believed to be extinct, were found alive. Ronald Brenner and Anthony Harmsworth, who set up the Official Loch Ness Monster Show in Drumnadrochit, are very upset by the 'fish theory'. 'That is one opinion among many,' they keep on saying.

For sure there is no shortage of theories. The modern era for the Loch Ness monster started in 1933 when the A82 was opened from Fort William to Inverness, running alongside the western shores of the lake. Before there were only legends: the lake, formed when the north of Scotland slid a hundred kilometres to the south-west, is four million years old. Gaelic legends talk of a monster by the name of Each Uisge. St Columba met it in 565 and prevented it from eating up one of the old inhabitants of the place, a Pict. Cromwell's soldiers, especially on their return from the tavern reported 'moving islands' on the waters. In 1933, with the new road built, crowds came to the shores and started seeing all sorts of things: heads, backs, fins and scales. In 1934, as the sightings increased, the *Daily Mail* dispatched a safari expert by the name of Weatherall to solve the mystery. A few days later, Mr Weatherall's moment of glory came, when he found a huge footprint. When questioned about the reason for his prompt success, his answer was that nothing was impossible to a man of his calibre. For its part *The Times* smelt a rat and said so. In the end the British Museum identified the footprint as belonging to a hippopotamus. The locals found out that it had been made with an umbrella stand in the shape of a hippopotamus' foot. Mr Weatherall kept quiet and a few days later announced that he had sighted another monster, this time looking like a seal. He was summoned back to London.

In the following years a certain number of pictures excited the public at large, while making the sceptics more sceptical. In the one known as the 'Surgeon's', because it was taken by a gynaecologist on holiday, you can see a head and a neck emerging from the waters, while in 'MacNab's picture' a huge something is swimming just below the ruins of Urquhart Castle. In 1960, Mr Tim Dinsdale, an aeronautical engineer, filmed a large animal swimming in the lake. Both NASA and the RAF inspected the film and approved it, thereby creating a lot of excitement. A Loch Ness Phenomenon Investigation Office was set up, and fanatics from all over the world came to conduct so-called 'scientific experiments'. Let's look at a few: an airship was flown over the lake, in the hope that an air survey would solve the mystery. It was already in the air when someone pointed out that, in the peaty waters of the lake, visibility stops one yard below the surface. Mr Dan Taylor went down in front of the cameras in his yellow submarine, the Viperfish. He was back in no time: at a depth of eight metres, he could not see a thing, the vessel was extremely noisy, very slow and could not be controlled. Two harpoons had been mounted on the Viperfish with a view to taking samples of tissue from the animal and carrying out a biopsy. The end result of the expedition was so disastrous that someone proposed to harpoon the director of the Investigation Office, but they didn't even do that.

There were other interesting attempts: in the seventies a school of Dolphins was trained to take a camera and sufficient lighting into the depths of the lake. The RSPCA complained that the animals would suffer in the muddy waters; the whole thing came to an end when the head dolphin had a heart attack during a training session and died. A few years before that, the mechanical monster used in the 1969 film, *The Private Life of Sherlock Holmes*, was towed in by the Pisces, a small submarine. It sank ingloriously. This event, it was pointed out, was not necessarily a disaster: at least now there is a monster at the bottom of the lake.

Today the search goes on around the whole of Loch Ness. We motored down the eastern road, which is longer and less crowded, and we came across entire families on the lookout for Nessie. This is how they spend their holidays: father stands behind his binoculars, mother is ready with the camera and the children take it in turns to sit on a folding chair and look straight into the dark waves. When we stopped the car and asked for news, they seemed very happy to share the delights of mounting guard over the lake with an amateur. An insurance broker from Glasgow, his eyes glued to binoculars, explained to us that Nessie hunting is an ideal weekend occupation: it is not expensive, it's out in the fresh air, and is relaxing because nothing ever happens. Children are the only problem: they get bored because they don't believe in the monster.

6

Up North

Sheffield: The Heroic Death of the Steel City

What is most striking about the collapse of Britain's northern cities is the sheer simplicity of the process and the enormity of its effects. The trouble afflicting the main industries has spread to other related businesses and all around the signs of a breakdown are only too apparent: deserted docks in Liverpool, ghettoes in Birmingham and here, in Sheffield, red brick steel-works with broken windows, industrial debris and 'For Sale' signs. I found these last particularly moving because it is obvious that in this part of the world, disasters are difficult commodities to trade.

You do not have to be an economist and you do not need to have read a lot on the subject either, to realise that something momentous happened here. You just have to motor along the 'lower Don valley' – that is the name of the local river – to figure out what Sheffield was like, and to see what it is like now. The streets with names such as Vulcan Road are like canyons in a wasteland of closed down steelworks. Hadfield Steel, Firth Brown, Jessop, Darwin-Balfour: they are all closed. Each factory had its pub where workers had a drink before and after shifts. When the factories went, the pubs went too, like the Alexandra Palace with its green walls and stained glass windows which was just below the Carlisle Works. Mr Lawrence Grimsdale, a retired schools

inspector, who came to Sheffield in 1955, showed us around.
'I used to take half an hour to cross this district twenty years
ago,' he says. 'Now there is no traffic, it takes me ten minutes:
it is so sad.' Looking out from Tinsley bridge at the start of
the motorway leading to Barnsley and Leeds, the only moving objects are bulldozers picking their way through
mountains of rubble and gypsies in their camps. A few miles
away, in Attercliffe and Brightside, two British Steel works
and a few related industrial concerns still function, but for
how long? The largest privately owned steelworks, the Sheffield Forgemasters, lost £16 million in one year. In Sheffield
and Rotherham – the nearby town with an economy based on
steel and coal as well – jobs have been cut from 60,000 to
25,000 in ten years. In 1967, Labour nationalised the steelworks; subsequent Tory governments sold them to the
private sector: today, ideological squabbles are totally irrel-
evant in the face of such a disaster. The explanation is very
straightforward. It comes from Irvine Patnick, one of the very
few local Conservatives: 'There is no need for all that much
steel in Great Britain and it is cheaper to import it from Japan
than to produce it on the spot.'

All that is left are the 'For sale' signs and the cheerful
coloured promotional leaflet which they insisted on charg-
ing us for at the Town Hall. There is also a glorious past:
Sheffield became the 'Steel City' in 1740 when Benjamin
Huntsman was able to produce steel of such an even quality
that tool manufacturing was radically improved. Mr Huntsman, the vast nearby coalfields and the proximity of the
North Sea, all contributed to Sheffield's rise. In the words
of the Reverend Alan Billings, the odd Marxist deputy
mayor: 'If we had not produced guns for the German Navy
in 1914 and had not manufactured steel for the English
Navy thirty years later, we would not be in this mess.'

Sheffield has also declined in the manufacturing of day to
day objects: after battleships, cutlery. Cutlery was produced
in another part of town, towards the centre, as an obvious
spin-off in the production of special alloys. Until recently

'Sheffield blades' were in use in kitchens all over the world, until the producers shot themselves in the foot. They thought that the label, 'Made in Sheffield', would beat any competition, so they started to import rough blades from the Far East, where they came cheap, and to dress them up with their registered trademark. The Japanese and the Koreans realised this was playing into their hands: today, 98 per cent of the world market for volume cutlery (which is inferior quality cutlery) is in their hands. As one of the people we spoke to put it, 'First the Japanese sent their cutlery to Sheffield to have it finished off, then they thought they could use it to finish Sheffield off.'

The enormity of the disaster, as much for the cutlery as the whole steel industry, are immediately evident. You don't even need to visit the recently opened industrial museum: you can see it all in the streets. If you want to understand what happened to the craftsmen who used to manufacture only scissor blades which were then assembled elsewhere, or what happened to those who only made carving knives, all you have to do is to visit the yards where there used to be five workshops, and now there is only one. Or look at what is left of Viners, the most famous steelworks: it was pulled down three years ago among the cheers of the local children.

Today, Sheffield hangs onto its last market niche: quality cutlery. In the centre of town next to travel agents offering cut price holidays to Tenerife and shop windows full of polyester jackets, there are still shops which only sell knives. There is Mrs Robinson, the owner of Sheffield Scene, for whom the motto is 'No Japanese cutlery'. When there are no more customers for the famous 'Kitchen Devils', she will close down.

Local politicians blame one another for this decline. The Town Council, which has been Labour-controlled for the past fifty years, is fed up with the Tory Government's 'short-sighted and deflationary policy'. The Tories reply that since local government has always been Labour-controlled, Labour must take the responsibility. In the words of the leader of the local Conservatives, Mr Irvine Patnick, 'Instead of flying the red flag on the Town Hall on Labour Day and twinning with Bulgarian cities, the Council should have declared Sheffield "a free enterprise zone": then we would not be in such a state.'

Mr Patnick is a short, talkative and very lively Jew. He gave up his day in the synagogue on Yom Kippur to come and talk to us about what his opponents have been up to. He had very clear ideas about the ruling Labour administration: in his words, 'Sheffield is the capital of the People's Socialist Republic of Yorkshire.' He called the Town Hall, 'our little Kremlin'. He showed us around the place, up stairs and along corridors, chatting away all the time, until we reached the roof and there with the town below us, where no one could overhear him, he blew his top: 'Do you know that the Labour Councillors turn up at Town Council meetings with sandals on like Jesus Christ and take their children and dogs along? And that two months ago, during my speech, the Town Councillor opposite me was breastfeeding her baby?' On our way downstairs again, he makes a face at a typist's bare feet and sighs whilst walking past the marble statue of the Catholic Duke of Norfolk, who was mayor in 1857.

According to Mr Patnick, Sheffield is falling to pieces. According to the Reverend Alan Billings, the deputy mayor with a dog collar (the sensible face of folly, for the Tories), the town is about to be born again. To bring that about, the City Council offers a lot of free services and spends more than it collects. This attitude, which has resulted in bitter quarrels with central government, has resulted, some say, in the town being abandoned to its own destiny. The only certainty is that the poor people living in council blocks behind the railway station are really poor. We went up there: from one point you can see where Sheffield ends and Derbyshire's green fields begin. From this vantage the town seems less ugly, but unnaturally quiet, and almost clean, with no smoke coming out of the chimneys. These blocks, which one architect with a warped sense of humour christened 'Hyde Park', were built when the town was bustling, dirty and wealthy. Now it has all changed. Only the girls in their white nylon stockings go down at night into town as they always have: in pairs, silently, with their arms folded across their chests.

Manchester: Nice memories and large loos

Of the numerous records it once held, Manchester now holds only one: it houses the 'longest lavatory in Europe'. This shouldn't be taken literally though; actually this is what the locals call the Arndale Centre, a shopping centre built in the seventies. It would be ugly enough on the outskirts of some American town, but here, right in the middle of what used to be 'the most exciting Victorian city', it is simply awful. At the *Manchester Evening News*, journalists have an interesting theory: they suggest that it's made from a huge block of cheese – it's the right shape and colour – and fell from the sky as a punishment for the town's sins.

Manchester, together with other towns in the north of England, must have sinned a lot to be visited with the terrible times of the last few years. Like Newcastle, Sheffield and Liverpool, Manchester is a casualty of the industrial revolution. Today, the North, which means approximately anything north of Birmingham, has higher unemployment, higher mortality rates, fewer home owners and a less nutritious diet than the South. Take the fifty wealthiest towns in Great Britain: forty are below a line from the Bristol Channel to the Wash, one hundred kilometres north of London. The first northern town on the list is Scottish: Aberdeen made it to nineteenth place thanks to North Sea Oil.

It sounds incredible, but Manchester really was an important city once. It was at the forefront of the Industrial Revolution in the last century, when the North caught up with London. At the end of the eighteenth century, 10 per cent of the British population lived in London, the centre for agricultural production and trade for England and Wales. Manchester invested in the textile industry, Sheffield special-ised in steel and Liverpool enlarged its port. In 1830 there were 185 mills in Manchester, 28 silk mills and scores of smaller industries with a very varied production, from Charles MacIntosh's waterproofs to Joseph Whitworth's spe-cial screws. In that year, the first steam railway was opened: the railways gradually took over from the canals, which had been built in the previous century. There was enough smoke and jobs for everyone. Brian Robson – who's not a footballer, but a Professor of Geography at Manchester University, quoted Yeats to describe those bustling times, 'All changed, changed utterly: A terrible beauty is born.'

We met him on a deserted campus, on a Friday afternoon. Mr Robson, the author of the pamphlet, *Where is the North*, explained that the decline of this part of Britain was the result of shortsightedness of the local businessmen at the beginning of the century. Their lack of innovation, together with the advent of the First World War, proved fatal to the region. Manchester declined from then on, along with the British manufacturing industry. In the past fifteen years, the rate of the decline has been staggering. Figures can be boring, but can help us to understand: while industrial output rose by 22 per cent between 1974 and 1984 in Italy, by 42 per cent in the United States and by 61 per cent in Japan, it fell by 4.3 per cent in Great Britain. In Manchester, the collapse really and truly started in 1979 when investment stopped. Today the population is down by one third compared with 1951; the unemployment rate is about 30 per cent and as much as 50 per cent for the under twenty-fives.

You can see the clearest signs of the upheaval in the centre. It looks as if the old Victorian town suddenly died and the new town was never born. One quarter of the houses, according to the housing officers themselves, is not up to standard, and a lot of buildings hastily put up in the sixties to clear slums (64,000 houses were pulled down in ten years), need massive repairs. Sewers have been a problem as well: they were built for a large population and for few vehicles. Now they are caving in under the sheer weight of traffic. After fifty accidents of this kind since 1979, the City Council now monitors the situation with the 'DDB', which stands for double decker bus. The strength of the sewers is measured by the number of buses which can motor over them without their breaking.

Of all the Manchester districts, the most depressing is Hume, just south of the centre beyond the railway line. It is a maze of tower blocks, which were built for factory workers, a rare sight in Britain. A huge block, looking like a strange animal on small legs, is better known as the 'bull ring'. No taxi driver will venture there at night. The streets in the centre of town, which ocasionally widen into vast carparks, offer strange sights as well. Buildings have been pulled down there, and nothing has been built in their place. The fact is that no one wants to be the first to settle in the deserted inner city. The Labour City Council, on the other hand, is opposed on ideological grounds to selling the land. When it does, it slaps a preservation order on it, thereby tying the hands of the developers. Those who had no choice but to remain in the centre, rent their homes and many do not pay their rents. Manchester City Council acknowledged sometime ago that it was owed £8,400,000 in uncollected rent. There are new industries, like electronics, which they say will save the town – the first computer was made in Manchester in 1949 – but they need space and they tend to go to the outskirts. The middle classes on the lookout for bigger homes have also moved out into suburbia and the shopping centres have gone after them.

As a result the town centre, with its wealth of memories and ugly buildings, has been left to the poor: the magnificent red brick warehouses in Whitworth Street, two hundred yards from the Italian Consulate, and the Arndale Centre, looking like an outsize public convenience. And finally, the arguable conversions: in Fennel Street the Corn and Produce Exchange has become the Pizzeria e Ristorante Vesuvio; the old railway station, a large showroom; and the Royal Exchange, an avant-garde theatre. As for Bombay Street and Bengali Street, you would think they had been recently bombed: perhaps they were, sometimes history can be explosive.

Liverpool and the girls at the Adelphi

If decay were a tourist attraction, as lakes and mountains are, and if you were interested in it, you ought to go to Liverpool. The town is exactly what Labour wants for Britain in order to be able to wax indignant with good reason. It is also what the Tory Party would rather not see: a dead port, a sick town and the promised regeneration which never seems to come about.

Anthony Steen was the very last Conservative MP for Liverpool. After his election in 1979, he founded, with the help of forty energetic housewives, Thatcher's, a tearoom where one can sit and eat apple pie under a portrait of the ex-Prime Minister. In the following election he stood again, but this time for a Devon constituency: he knew full well that in Merseyside he stood no chance. Today, there are six MPs for Liverpool, five Labour and one Liberal Democrat. The great pride and joy of the town was its football teams, Liverpool and Everton: the Heysel Stadium disaster (1985) and the events of Hillsborough (1989) have cast a cloud on them as well.

All this does not mean that Liverpool has no charm. It certainly has. It is dying the British way – languidly and with feeling – but it is certainly dying. Forty years ago, it was one of the most important commercial ports in the world, and eighty years ago it was the second city of the Empire. Now it is only important in our outdated Italian Touring Club 'Green Guide': we looked at the deserted

Mersey with a wry smile and read: 'This is a very busy trading centre for cotton, timber, grain, fruit, textiles and machinery.' The truth is that when trading links with America came to an end, Liverpool was unable to become an oil port like Rotterdam, and Britain's entry into the EEC tipped the scales in favour of locations on the Channel. In the south-east, unemployment is less than 9 per cent, up here it is as much as thirty. And while in the south-east you may still find some odd jobs to supplement the £30 a week dole, here the unemployed hang around from dawn to dusk.

In a nutshell, the problem with Liverpool is that it is folding up. We could see it straight away as our train entered Lime Street station: the buildings, all reminiscent of a great past, 'are set out higgledy-piggledy like the irregular front teeth of some of the locals', as Mario Praz noted. At mid morning the traffic was minimal, as in some East European towns, the shops uninviting and the people shabbily dressed. By the port, all there was to see were the chains used for African slaves as they waited to be shipped over to America. Cunard has moved to London, leaving behind its vast premises. The Irish Steamship Company discontinued the ferry service to Belfast when it realised that no one was boarding it. Next, it will be the turn of the small ferry boat linking the two sides of the estuary. The Mersey cuts through the town: to the north the centre, to the south Birkenhead, where the children used to go to swim and to watch American warships during the last war. The Ferry Boat Committee, under the chairmanship of an insurance broker, Mr Maurice Packman, was set up to save it. In the last ten years, he said, Liverpudlians have seen their town wither away: this is the last straw.

As a matter of fact people here are fascinated by the Mersey estuary and by water in general. The Merseyside Development Corporation realised it pretty quickly: it was flooded with enquiries when still in the process of converting the Albert Docks wharfs into small flats. These buildings, which are now completed, are the pride of the town: on Sundays entire families go there to sit outside in the wind, the fathers explaining to their children that there is still hope for Merseyside: just what Government officials and members of the Royal Family say over and over as well, but with less conviction, when they come all the way to Liverpool for short visits.

Along the rest of the river the landscape is very different: empty wharves, as tall as cathedrals, with smashed window panes. Nowadays, Liverpool harbour processes a mere ten million tons, 4 per cent of what Rotterdam processes, and almost all the goods are shipped across to Seaforth on the other side of the Irish Sea. Down in the port only the pubs – the Dominion, the Victoria and the Rule Britannia – remind one that things used to be different. The Baltic Fleet is one of the most famous: it was built ages ago in the shape of a ship to look out on the other ships on the river. The inner city is a little further away: half pulled down buildings, scruffy little houses and a lot of waste land waiting for someone to come along with the cash. In the Soviet-style *Liverpool Echo* headquarters, they told us about the Environment Minister's visit: they showed him around for a while and eventually he acknowledged that conditions were appalling in the centre. Government inaction has gone hand in hand with the arrogant attitude of the local Labour Council under Derek Hatton. Mr Hatton, well-known as a sharp dresser, was recently expelled from the party for his links with the leftist organization Militant. Neither he, nor his followers, would accept spending limits imposed by Central Government. They wanted more public money, and of course there was none.

Overlooking the river, falling to pieces and neglected, and yet almost beautiful, Toxteth sums it all up. There were serious race riots here in 1981, and every year since, though not so violent. On one occasion, the mob burnt down an art-nouveau theatre, the Rialto: just one more of a long list of memories. Catherine Street, with its prostitutes, is not very far away. 'Maggie Mae' of Rod Stewart fame, used to live there. Even that business is suffering: on Sunday mornings, their day of rest, prostitutes meet at Peter Kavanagh's to talk of the good old times when Polish sailors would climb all the way up to Toxteth, whereas nowadays the girls have to go down to the harbour when a ship puts in. The Philharmonic pub is the place for opera lovers. The gents' toilets are so beautiful with coloured ceramics, that on Tuesdays ladies are allowed in. Here too, they assured me that Liverpool has become the capital of 'another England', as David Sheppard, the local Anglican bishop calls it, when he gets worked up in his sermons.

If you were not convinced by statistics and the deserted docks, a visit to 'Beatles City' will make it clear to you that Liverpool is going through a bad patch. It is a museum of a kind situated in Seel Street, but hardly anyone ever visits it. At the entrance, a coloured teenager sells scarves and tee shirts, or rather would sell them if anyone wanted to buy them. Inside, you are treated to sixties films and a piped 'Love me do', in a dark tunnel. Now the museum is going to close for five months in the winter. Then if there are still no visitors, everything from John Lennon's first guitar, to Ringo Starr's Mini Morris with an enlarged boot to fit the drum kit into, is to be sold to the Japanese who have already showed an interest.

Another landmark of Liverpool's grand decadence is the Adelphi. In 1983 the hotel was sold by British Rail to a private group who tried to restore it to its former Edwardian splendour by putting in an abundance of mirrors and stuccoes. When the Adelphi was opened in 1914, it was one of the five most beautiful hotels in the world. On the lower floors, rooms were decorated in the style of the luxury transatlantic liners with extravagant bathrooms. In those days people stayed at the Adelphi before going on board, and later Harold Wilson spent Election nights there. Now you can find a cartoon strip in the lift offering discounts for dirty weekends with local girls who want a bit of sex and comfort once in a while, and cannot remember what the Adelphi was like only twenty years ago, and who could not care less.

It rains in Glasgow on Italia House

If you happen to be in Glasgow on a rainy day – which is not difficult, it rains every day – you ought to have a look at Italia House. For a start, it gives you shelter, but it also gives you an insight into Scotland's present problems and into Italy's melancholy past. Italia House is a time machine: in this Victorian building at 22, Park Circus, in the middle of Kelvingrove Park, you can see people with ties and jackets which have not been around in Italy for twenty years. Some of them support Naples Football Club and love Maradona, but still remember fondly Faustinho Cane, the Brazilian footballer, who could kick the ball so accurately and in whose honour children were taken to the stadium with their faces blackened with shoe polish.

The chairman of Italia House comes from Barga in Tuscany. He showed us around the cold disused rooms: of the original three hundred and fifty members, very few bother to turn up and fewer still pay their subs. The underground disco is a blue catacomb full of dust; two Salvation Army officers, in full uniform, were eating in the plush red velvet restaurant, while the function rooms for 'entertainment, wedding receptions, dinner dances and all sorts of parties', according to the Souvenir Brochure, were closed down to cut the heating bill. Over a drink, they explained to me that the place was set up in 1935 by the Fascists, confiscated by the British authorities in 1939 and given back in 1946. Italia House, according to the Chairman, did well in the fifties when Glasgow 'was black with soot and birds did not sing, they coughed.' When the birds stopped coughing, things went from bad to worse. 'The Italians are all in the Fish and Chips trade, which is the poor man's food: when the poor ran out of money, we Italians ran into trouble.'

And there is no doubt about that: poor people in Glasgow have been through terrible times indeed. For a start, you should know that every single industry has had to cut jobs; traditional industries, like shipyards, steelworks and textile factories now employ half the number of workers they did in 1971. At the beginning of the century there were twenty-three shipyards along the Clyde and one in every four ships in the world was built there, including all the Cunard liners – now the figure is one in one hundred and thirty.

In those days Glasgow had the advantage of facing the open sea; clippers with their loads of tobacco could get to America much faster than from London and were not under the threat of attack from privateers. Glasgow has not moved: markets have. The town around which half the Scottish population live is a 'depressed zone', the only other one in Scotland is Dundee. The Tory Government puts the money in; in return the Glaswegians despise it and vote Labour: the City Council has always been Labour and so are the majority of MPs. In 1922, at the time of the rise of Fascism in Italy, the 'Red Clydesiders' were at the height of their fame. They were ten public speakers who subsequently became Labour MPs: their popular following was such that they were able to turn the town against Lloyd George and forced him to move in the army. One of them, Harry McShane, became secretary to John MacLean, the first local consul appointed by the Bolsheviks. At the age of ninety-four, Mr McShane is still a convinced Marxist: 'That woman [Margaret Thatcher] thinks she is Adam Smith. Every man is a capitalist: daft stuff, son, daft stuff.'

Everything has been tried in Glasgow to achieve Mr McShane's Marxist vision. They cleaned up the Gorbals with its poverty, bad language and prostitution – but they left the council estates built all round the centre in the fifties. These estates keep Glasgow at the top of the list of the most violent cities in Europe. We decided to take a taxi there on a Sunday afternoon. The driver, a well-built man, spelt out immediately all the streets where he would not go for fear of having his windows smashed ('They hide behind those concrete walls, the bastards, and hurl stones at anything which moves.').

Touring the centre of town clockwise, we first of all saw Possilpark, which looked from a distance like a single concrete block. As we got closer, we saw that there were several buildings, all equally ugly, stinking staircases, graffiti on the walls and strange passageways. Anything could happen here, so they say: not long ago four boys forced their way into the home of a mentally handicapped girl, raped her and printed the walls blue with their hands. It is easy to imagine such nightmares taking place in such surroundings. Further on is Springburn, where British Steel Engineering used to be: the police station is a bunker and we saw a billboard advising us to 'invest in gold'. At Roystonhill there is a fishmarket and a solitary pub which opens at 7 am. Young men drive around in old black and red Morris Marinas and wait for something to happen, just as in some towns in the south of Italy: the same looks, the same elbows sticking out of the windows, the same music blaring from the car radio. This part of Glasgow has a strong Irish flavour, and it is where IRA terrorists go underground when they arrive from Ireland. If those were the dwellings that the Bauhaus architects dreamed about for the working classes at the time of the Weimar Republic, I would prefer the small tidy cottages of the nineteenth-century middle classes.

Fortunately, Glasgow has something else to offer. Change is in the air. The local council has launched a campaign to improve the image of the city in the style of 'I love New York'. Billboards, badges, buses, all proclaim 'Glasgow is miles better.' We do not know what Glasgow is better than – Ankara, Belgrade, or simply Edinburgh. The campaign at least got people talking, as they couldn't decide whether it was a laudable initiative, or whether they had simply gone mad in the Town Hall. The university is ancient, silent and clean. The city centre slopes down from West George Street and has its regular number of drunkards who are sick on the pavement on Saturday nights, but it could be worse. In Ulster, Catholics and Protestants murder each other: here they have a good fight after football matches at Park Head or Ibrox Park. In the olden days, the Protestants made the money from the tobacco trade and it was the Catholics, either from Ireland or the Highlands, who would unload the ships.

Another piece of good news is that the jobs which were being lost in the manufacturing industry (two thousand a month at the beginning of the seventies), are being recreated in the service industries: in banking, insurance and in more recent developments such as electronics (there are two hundred such industries in Scotland). People who have good jobs, don't want to know about the depressing suburbs, they want to bring about the social revival of the city ('the Berlin effect', in the words of Jim Murdoch, a young Public Law lecturer). Therefore, around the local BBC headquarters and near the university a score or so of sophisticated French restaurants have appeared, where you can eat minute quantities of food for a lot of money. They are called 'Lautrec's', 'Geltrude's wine bar', or 'La bonne auberge'. In Ashton Lane, at the 'Ubiquitous Chip', you can eat Scottish grouse in a sort of greenhouse, surrounded by beautiful fair-haired, well-dressed young ladies, smiling and chatting quietly together: a rare sight north of London. From there Glasgow looks hopeful and very self confident, the East End suburbs and the closed down yards seem miles away. It is hardly surprising that the people from Italia House, who take pride in having been photographed ages ago with an Italian President of the Republic and worry about the future of the fish and chips trade, are never seen there.

Blackpool: kiss-me-quick in spite of the sea

Until recently, in the north of England, people had two hobbies: maligning southerners and going on holiday to Blackpool. Unfortunately for Blackpool, only the former occupation is still thriving because it does not cost anything. As a result, there are fewer and fewer customers in this cold resort overlooking the Irish Sea. Miners and their families still come from nearby Yorkshire: apparently Blackpool provides enough beer and illuminations for them. In the autumn, party and trade union conferences still fill the place up for a week at a time. But that is not enough, nor is it enough to be called 'The Las Vegas of Lancashire', the town of one-arm bandits at ten pence a go and of three thousand bed and breakfast houses, seven pounds a night with sea view.

The reasons for Blackpool's decline are very obvious, they will tell you when they eventually answer your questions. The north has been poor for a long time; poor with much unemployment. Poor unemployed people have no money for holidays. Those who have a bit saved will go to Spain: every year eight million people go off on package tours. They come back a fortnight later with a sombrero and sunburn. You can have a week in Benidorm for as little as £99 all inclusive. Blackpool cannot compete with that.

Before giving in, Blackpool tried everything. It cultivated the image of the working class sea-resort, British through and through, smelling of fish and chips and suntan lotion: the working classes had no reason to go to Spain where they were herded like cattle. They should keep on coming to Blackpool instead, as they had done since 1770, to drink beer and to eye the girls on the Golden Mile, the promenade, which is only five hundred yards long in spite of its name. A few years ago, the local tourist office went as far as publishing a pamphlet bearing the title 'Come to Costa Notta Lotta'. There are now more amusements in the 450 foot-high tower; striptease is allowed in the clubs along the promenade (officially it is family entertainment). A lot of effort has been put into discouraging bathing in the sea, which is certainly a good idea. (In the 1988 Water Report, the Ministry for the Environment stated that the sea at Blackpool did not meet the minimum EEC standards.) The Tourist Office even invented a 'Pickled Cabbage Festival' to entice German clients, but the Germans were not going to travel a thousand miles to the north in search of the sun.

Thanks both to those brilliant ideas and to price cuts, Blackpool is still alive. In August, they say at the Tourist Office, five hundred thousand eggs are cracked every morning at the bed and breakfasts, so someone must be eating them. As far as the future is concerned, it depends on the economic climate of the whole region. If it gets better and if new industries, services and electronics replace the old ones, then the exodus to the south which has been particularly important in Greater Manchester and Merseyside, will be stemmed. Mentalities might even change. The CBI described it as 'discouragement coupled with a certainty that it is always somebody else's responsibility: it is up to the south, Europe, the Japanese, it is never up to the northerners themselves.'

In Lancashire they are not convinced of that. The north is not doing well they say, because the south-east would only be too happy to get rid of it and let it drift off into the Atlantic. There are small things which would help: why not allow children into pubs with their parents for instance? At the moment, the husband goes in for a drink, while wife and children look in through the window like characters from Dickens.

Each spring they say at Blackpool, 'next summer will either make it or break it.' Each summer the 'Las Vegas of Lancashire' sells the same dirty picture postcards, the same Kiss-me-Quick caps. In the discount stores the same girls in stiletto heels, with their half-drunk boyfriends look at electrical applicances for their future homes. London is two hundred and fifty miles away: the capital of another nation. On the promenade in the local Madame Tussaud's, Margaret Thatcher has been replaced by Boy George: that is what they think of the Government.

7

Quirks

Plumbing the depths of the Soul

Some enlightened individuals are convinced that for a visitor the single most fascinating thing in Great Britain is either the Royal Family, or Mrs Thatcher, or Scottish castles. That is not true at all. What mesmerises foreigners are some extraordinary British habits, which have defeated even the best brains in Europe. No one, for instance can give a satisfactory explanation as to why in British hand basins, there are two separate taps, one for hot water and one for cold water, usually fixed to the corners of the basin, so that the choice is between getting your hands scorched under the hot tap, or frozen under the cold one, while washing is practically impossible. It is such an ingrained habit that when the Government ran a vast advertising campaign in the press to encourage energy saving, it came up with the picture of a sink which in Italy would be a collector's item.

From the mystery of the hand basin to the mystery of the bidet. The reason why the British persist in ignoring its existence has been endlessly debated. Protestant puritanism has been offered as an explanation: the bidet is not popular because it is connected to ever-intimate washing. I do not think I agree with that: much more likely bidets are shunned because English people know that once they have one installed, they must use it. And in spite of all efforts to prove to the contrary, I think I have detected a certain disinclination when it comes to washing. True enough, figures tend to prove the opposite: apparently no European country uses as much water between 7am and 9am as Great Britain, but these are British statistics. Besides, people might simply enjoy the sound of running water and since half British families have a pet, it is possible that it is the pet that gets a wash in the morning.

The troubled relationship of the British with their bathrooms goes back a long way. We have no intention of delving into the history of hydraulics. Let's just mention that in the Middle Ages the British went to extraordinary lengths to avoid talking openly of toilets: the nobility and the clergy used periphrases such as necessarium and garderobe. In rich houses and in castles, garderobes were eked out in the thickness of the walls or else they jutted out, discharging into the empty space below. Consequently moats, which had been built around castles for defence purposes, became offensive at least for the attackers' sense of smell. In 1313 Sir William de Norwico had a wall built to conceal such discharges. Many 'secret rooms' and 'private chapels' in castles and mansions were really toilets. At Abingdon Pigotts, not far from Royston, the hole in the middle of the 'altarstone' looks decidedly suspicious.

In Victorian times the course of history almost changed as a consequence of poor sanitation. After a stay at Londesborough Lodge, near Scarborough, the Prince of Wales and members of his party went down with typhoid: His Highness survived, but the Earl of Chesterfield and his valet died. The nation was badly shaken: the heir to the throne had almost succumbed to the bad sewers of the county. It is said that after his illness, the Prince of Wales publicly gave his backing to the crusade for better sanitation and told his future subjects that he would have liked to be a plumber, had he not been born a prince.

In that case, he would have been very busy indeed in the following years. After the First World War, when Great

Britain started buying vast quantities of enamelled appliances, it did not plumb them into decent bathrooms. The nineteenth-century middle-class terrace houses only had a couple of proper rooms on each of their three or four floors: it did not even cross people's minds to use one of them for something as optional as a bathroom. Furthermore, during the war, hosts of servants found better paid jobs in factories, so they did not come back to their basements at the end of it. Terraced houses were divided up into maisonettes and studio flats, and toilets ended up on the landing. And with the resonance provided by the stair well, every one was kept up to date with every one else's bowel movements.

Things have not changed much today. Just take a walk around Bayswater, focusing your attention on the backs of houses, and you can see bathrooms built in incredible places. A visit to the beautiful white houses in the crescents of Notting Hill will show you that for generations the owners could not care two hoots about their bathrooms. They either ended up on the landing, or in the attic, or under the stairs or in a corner of the bedroom. Because of those architectural acrobatics, windows in British bathrooms are an optional extra, like jacuzzis. Almost everywhere you can still see the so-called 'plumber's delight', a glass shelf below the mirror, resting on two supports which are too far apart. You just touch it and it is in the sink in a thousand pieces.

Apart from the problems with taps which we mentioned above, there is also a dearth of good showers, and water closets do not seem to be terribly reliable. 'How many WCs do actually work when flushed the first time?' asks Lawrence Wright straight from the heart in *Clean and Decent* 1961. The Duchess of York herself brought the argument into the open during a visit to Los Angeles in 1988, to the great delight of her American hosts. They expected anything but a complete account of Windsor Castle's plumbing from a member of the Royal Family.

If bathrooms were clean, one might even say that they

are part of the charm of an English home – that is, if you really enjoy being the last person in a windowless bed and breakfast's bathroom. But we think that because they do not think much of the room itself, the British see no point in going to great lengths to clean and maintain it. We can still remember with a mixture of horror and nostalgia what happened to us during the first months of our stay in Britain when we were living with some friends in Clapham. We noticed that the inside of the bath tub was mossy green, but knowing that most pre war appliances were white, we asked, 'Is it possible that some rare lichens are growing there?' The answer was invariably the same: 'Do not worry, the tub is green anyway.' Unconvinced, we carried out an experiment with sponge and detergent on a Sunday afternoon while our hosts were out: it turned out after a few hours' scrubbing, that the tub was actually white. Now our hosts are sure that we have replaced it and that on the Continent we have an obsession for cleanliness bordering on madness.

Italians have always been perplexed by all that. They have just about grasped that you enter a bathroom in Great Britain at your own risk – everywhere but in smart hotels, where everything is available, bidets included, but not windows – when they realise that more surprises are in store around the country. A headmaster from northern Italy wrote to us some time ago enquiring about 'English girls with no stockings on in the winter and navy-blue legs' whom I had mentioned in an article. I decided therefore to investigate the matter further.

I questioned some barelegged English friends of mine – I have others who do wear stockings – and the answer was that they were not cold, therefore they did not need any stockings. We probed further: 'How come that your legs are blue if you are not cold?' The answer was that it can happen anyway whether you are freezing or not. Perhaps it was a way of saving money, we thought: but even this is not true. British girls go dancing barelegged and spend the equivalent of five pairs of tights in an evening. Further investigation produced the following results: middle-class girls wear stockings more often than working class ones; girls from the south often more than girls from the north and London transvestites more often than anyone else.

We also know – and this could be another reason – that British girls think that their bare blue legs are attractive and even more so with the awful red mock leather shoes they like to put on their feet. It is also worth considering that generation upon generation of teenage girls at boarding schools, having to choose between thick woolly stockings and bare legs, opted for the latter since they were not allowed nylon stockings, and now they have got used to it. Otherwise it must be a way to keep close to nature: in Britain girls go around barelegged and men run in parks in their underwear as soon as the sun pops out. But in the end perhaps the answer is that British girls are miles behind their continental peers: they dress like Italian and French girls in the post-war years. So round about 2020 they might discover tights and one day the whole country might even use bidets and swivelling water taps. But I know, this is a pipe dream.

How I fell in love with an armchair

For some Englishmen, clubs are like mistresses: Italian and French husbands fall for another woman when they want to get away from their wives, the British fall for a leather armchair. And like mistresses, clubs do not come cheap and go out of fashion. Clubs are thriving in London these days. With AIDS around, sex has become a very dangerous sport: the British gentleman is ever more inclined to opt for a leather armchair. In old clubs, where members are proud of the long waiting lists and of the prosperous budgets, menus have been changed: it is imitation French cuisine now, instead of roast beef and Yorkshire pudding. Membership has changed in line with menus: retired colonels are still there but in the company of well-mannered and well-paid young men, often from the City, who think that paying £400 a year for a bit of style is quite reasonable.

Before tackling the reasons for the revival of gentlemen's clubs, it is interesting to examine why they were successful in the first place when they were established in the middle of the last century. Anthony Lejeune and Malcolm Lewis, in *The Gentlemen's Clubs of London*, spoke of the 'need for wealthy Englishmen to get away from women and domestic worries'. It looks convincing enough, especially when you consider the trouble they went to keep wives out. In the clubs, gentlemen wanted to read without being interrupted, smoke without being castigated, drink without being looked at askance and talk politics to an interested audience. In other words they did not want their wives there. For a century they have lived in fear that women would be allowed in. It is said that Sir Bindon Blood woke up from his nap with a fright when he overheard the swoosh of a skirt next to him. He opened his eyes and saw the Club secretary showing Queen Mary around. He went back to his slumber saying loudly to his neighbour, 'This is the snowball that turns into an avalanche, my friend.'

People brought up in public schools find themselves very at ease in clubs. Bruce Scramblers, secretary and historian of the Traveller's Club, 106 Pall Mall, has no illusion over the lifestyle of the founder members in 1820. 'They used to have late lunches, visit their tailors, sneak out of the back door and spend the rest of the afternoon in Savile Row's brothels. They came back in the evening to eat, drink and play cards.' A very widely accepted explanation of the success of various clubs such as White's and the Reform is the following: gentlemen did not go to clubs to meet their peers, they went there to be left in peace, especially by their peers. For this reason the Royal Automobile Club in Pall Mall, cruelly renamed The Chauffeurs' Arms and always overcrowded, is looked at with mild disdain, while the Hurlingham is not even considered a real club: it is no more than a meeting point for foreigners when Harrods is closed. In the heyday of the Royal Automobile Club, it is said that a retired army colonel turned up with this famous statement. 'I had a full life and I intend to end it in peace. I have come here to die and my only wish is to pass away peacefully and quietly in the comfort of this old armchair.' Apparently his wishes were fulfilled.

Although there are still a number of old gentlemen of this kind dozing in clubs' reading rooms, clubs have undergone a profound change for a variety of reasons. For a start, by a process of natural selection, some financially less viable clubs went under in the seventies when London was less rich and more socialist. There has been a redistribution of members: for instance the Naval and Military – better known as 'In and Out' – has taken over the Cowdray, the Canning and the United Services (better known as The Senior). Members of the St James's joined Brook's and the Cavalry and the Guards have merged into the Cavalry and Guards. It now has a membership of three thousand two hundred, mainly from the army: the yearly sub is two days' pay for captains and above, and one day for other ranks.

Women are another explanation for the clubs' success. Until recently they were only allowed through the kitchen windows on their way to the members' bedrooms upstairs. The Reform (104 Pall Mall) has been admitting lady members since 1981 on the strength of its liberal traditions. It is the only one of the big clubs to have done so. Other clubs, but not all of them, allow them in as guests. Brook's is open to ladies after 6pm, which has apparently allowed the restaurant to show a profit again. Wives, girl friends, and secretaries are allowed in the Naval and Military, by separate entrance if properly dressed. At the Army and Navy and at the Reform there is even a Ladies' room. At the Garrick (15 Garrick Street), which has an excellent reputation for its food, and where lawyers, journalists and the like meet, ladies are welcome. This is not the case for the Athaeneum, the den of the clergy establishment. Rudyard Kipling obviously did not find the place very exciting. 'It is like a cathedral in between services,' he said. There are other anecdotes on the same lines about it. For instance, it is said this announcement appeared in the press some time ago: 'The Athaeneum has been reopened today, members are back in their original places.' On his first visit, Sir James Barrie, of Peter Pan fame, asked an octogenarian biologist slumped in an armchair to direct him to the dining room. The old man burst into tears: he had been a member for fifty years and no one had yet spoken to him.

Besides reorganisation and allowing ladies in, there are plain economic reasons for the present success of clubs. For a start the management has changed. Gone are the retired colonels who had waged war successfully all over the world, but were ripped off by the traders; they have been replaced by young managers with an appropriate training. Thanks to them the big clubs are almost all in the black: the Reform – where Gladstone, Palmerston, Asquith, Churchill and Lloyd George used to come for a drink – made a profit of £190,000 in 1986. With the rocketing cost of lodging and eating in London, many members have realised that the old 'gentlemen's club' is a bargain. Here are the charges: £400 annual sub, £10 for a lunch, £20 for dinner and £25 for a single room. It is Margaret Thatcher of course who taught the upper class the advantages of being thrifty. Her Government also made this clear: there was no spare cash to help clubs to maintain their often magnificent premises. The club committees saw the writing on the wall and got organised; some say they should even encourage members to vote Tory out of sheer gratitude, but as they already do so anyway, it is not necessary.

Clubs in Pall Mall and in St James's may have changed, but they have not become Holiday Inns. They have sorted out their finances, while keeping their peculiarities. The oldest one, dating from 1693, is 'White's' originally a patisserie belonging to a Mr Bianco, an Italian who preferred to use his name in the English translation. They do not seriously think of allowing women in. At the Garrick they do not like members to read the paper in the dining room: not long ago a member had his copy of *The Times* set on fire while he was doing just that. At the Reform prospective members must declare their intention of pursuing Liberal aims: some years ago Arkadij Maslennikov, the London correspondent of *Pravda*, said that he would, but no one believed him. At the Traveller's in the old days, members had to prove that they had been at least 500 miles away from London as the crow flies. Today's members, a lot of them from the nearby Foreign Office, are upset when American guests refuse to leave bags and hats in the cloakroom, for fear of having them stolen. That cannot possibly happen in a gentlemen's club, but if it did, there is an elegant way to get out of it. Not long ago there was the following notice at the entrance of one of the Pall Mall clubs: 'Would whoever might inadvertently have taken a blue cashmere coat, and left a lightweight jacket in its place, please report in confidence to the secretary.'

To please Wodehouse

Great Britain has a very easy-going approach to the 'servant problem' reminiscent of the way in which problems with the empire were tackled. When subjects protested, they were renamed 'Citizens of the Commonwealth', but not much has changed; when in the sixties servants did not like to be called servants, they were upgraded to 'domestic help', but there again there was no change of substance. The sheer number of servants has decreased for a variety of reasons: a collective guilt complex, the widespread use of domestic electric appliances, and the possibility of letting basements to foreigners taken in by names like lower ground floor or garden flat. That has marked the end of a typical British game called 'Upstairs Downstairs': downstairs staff gossiped and smoked cigars, while their masters stayed upstairs where they could surround themselves with the silver and try and produce an heir without being interrupted.

In the eighties the nouveaux riches, having got over the shock of their recent wealth, started looking out for butlers, maids, cooks and gardeners. Of course style, number of servants, relationship, and wages have all changed. Twenty-three year-old city whiz-kids who can now afford a butler rely on him when it comes to deciding on the number of buttons on jacket sleeves, a bit like Bertie Wooster and Jeeves. P. G. Wodehouse would be fascinated by all this.

Let's begin with a few figures. The 1851 Census showed that servants were the largest body in London, second only to farm workers, and that they were also the largest trade union in the capital. London had 121,000 servants, half of whom were under twenty-five, at a time when only six other towns in Great Britain had a larger total population. Eighty years later in 1931, in the whole country 1,382,000 were still employed in that sector. The latest statistic from the Department of Employment in 1986 gives a total of 181,000 servants for Great Britain, 159,000 women and 22,000 men. The figure, which includes nannies, au pairs and charladies, is total nonsense: for tax purposes nannies become assistants to professional people and to get away from NHS contributions French au pairs are officially 'guests', though sometimes they work like slaves.

Butlers have benefited most from the 'revival of Victorian values' (whatever that means) and from the new wealth in the City. The 'Great English Butler' has become administrator, sommelier, chauffeur, personal assistant and, more important, he pockets £1500 a month on top of board and lodging. Ivor Spencer, who set up Ivor Spencer's School for Butlers in the south of London in 1981, maintains that pupils who have successfully completed the four-term course are so heavily in demand that they can choose their employer and his nationality. At the school they learn to serve champagne, to have clean breath and not to stare at their mistresses when serving early morning tea. It is interesting to notice and certainly a sign of the changing times that the school does not train butlers only, it trains masters as well, so that in due course they will know how to handle them. Every four months the whole lot of them, pupils, future employers and teachers, move over to the Dorchester Hotel for practicals.

Nannies are doing well too. They are in great demand with ladies who do not want to give up their careers or their spare time. The girls, who do not look like Mary Poppins any longer, are of two sorts: professional and beginners. The former have been trained at the Norland Nursery Training College in Hungerford: they make as much as £125 a week and are in great demand. The only problem with them is that they are extremely competent so they end up despising their mistresses.

Beginners set other problems for the average family. Either they are upper-class young ladies looking for a pastime, in which case they will take objection to their employers' table manners, or they are girls from the North looking for a job in London, and they are homesick, and spend their spare time crying over their boy friends' photos. Some of them give up and go back to Liverpool, some get over it, ask for more money and go professional. That procedure is well known to Italian ladies who move to London. They advertise in *The Lady* and embark on the daunting task of interviewing the candidates; some are lucky and get an English girl with a gentle disposition and a love of children, some who are not very familiar with British accents and behaviour, end up entrusting their offspring to viragoes who plot to steal the family silver or run away with a night club doorman. A full-time nanny in London makes about £75 a week, on top of full board and lodging. People who want to save money hire foreign nannies. As Filipinos and other Asian girls do not get their working permits very easily, girls from EEC countries like Spain and Portugal have been doing very well.

Au pairs are also in demand. Australians and New Zealanders are the most sought after. Apparently they work harder than French or Italian girls and they complain less. Swedish teenagers are always popular with husbands, therefore wives have wiped them off almost completely. By law an au pair should only mind the children and do some light domestic duties, and should receive full board and lodging and about £25 a week. In practice things hardly ever work out that way. Some families of long liberal tradition and suffering from a hidden guilt complex, are far too kind: Auberon Waugh recalls a French au pair tired of being treated with kid gloves, who shouted: 'Monsieur, vous avez peur de me commander!' Other families instead seem to forget that those girls have come mainly to learn the language and treat them like skivvies from early in the morning to late at night. Hardly ever, on the other hand, are au pairs treated according to Mrs Beaton's instructions in her *Cookery and Household Management*: 'A lady must not forget the importance of the well being, both physical and moral of the people who live under her roof. As for girls it is her duty to keep herself discretely informed about the people they consort with. She must set a curfew, normally at 9pm and it is her duty to put the young people in touch with a representative of their religion or with a recognised organisation such as the Association of Young Christian Women.'

Mrs Beaton would have been very surprised by another development on the domestic service scene in Great Britain: the agencies who look after single yuppies. The best known is Mops & Brooms, which was recently praised by the *Financial Times*. The relationship between the maids dispatched by the agency and the young men is rather strange: their paths never cross. She comes when he is at work and picks up his dirty socks. For his part the yupped – yuppie employing domestic staff – does not put her in touch with a representative of her religion. He leaves a cheque instead.

What matters is the season

Few things are more riveting than the sight of English people playing games. They have always been very good at it: not only have they invented a good deal of modern sports, but they have also introduced some interesting variants: gentlemen's clubs for the winter – middle-aged men drinking, smoking and gambling at a safe distance from their wives – and the season for the summer.

To make up for an atrocious winter and an unreliable spring, the British concentrate all their open-air rituals in the so-called warm season. The main ones are Wimbledon (June to beginning of July), Glyndebourne (May to August), Ascot (June), the Henley Regatta and Buckingham Palace garden parties, both in July. For each of these there is a series of unwritten rules about which the British, who know them, get very worked up whereas foreigners, who do not know them, live in terror of getting them wrong and normally do. Ask a silly question or clap at the wrong time and the British connoisseur will immediately know that you are not from Richmond but from Mantua or Aix-en-Provence. For the visiting journalist the hordes of foreigners who seem to be able to get in anywhere and the boisterous noveaux riches, who made the most of ten years of Thatcherism, are fascinating new developments; for the old aristocracy a good reason for staying at home.

Let's start with Wimbledon. However exciting tennis may be, it is not the sole driving force behind the crowds entering the All England Lawn Tennis & Croquet Club, London SW19. Each year four hundred thousand spectators munch their way through eight tons of salmon, four tons of steak, pour down their throats twelve thousand bottles of champagne, 75,200 pints of beer, 300,000 cups of coffee and tea, and plough their way through five tons of sweets, 190,000 sandwiches, 23 tons of strawberries and 1,400 gallons of fresh cream. Strawberries and cream are the essence of

Wimbledon: people eat them out of a sense of duty whether they want them or not.

Then there are the special enclosures. The Royal box on the centre court is the most exclusive. The Members' Enclosure, strenuously defended by guards in blue blazers, overlooks as many as twelve courts. At the south end of the grounds are the marquees of the big corporations which can house about thirty people each. The big businesses (ICI, Barclays, IBM, Heinz) are in numbers 1 to 24: it can cost as much as £100,000 to look after friends and clients. Upper middle-class trade and industry is on the northern side. All the others have put up their tents outside the grounds, and there are so many of them that Wimbledon Borough Council had to intervene to stop the place becoming a camp-site.

Big business has not yet pitched its tents at Glynebourne on the Sussex Downs, but they would if they could. English people in evening dress have been coming here for the past fifty years to listen to good music and to picnic: the organisers like to think that it is an opera with picnics in the intervals, but it is more of a picnic with an opera thrown in. As usual the ritual is what matters: you set out for Lewes from Victoria and you start drinking even before the train has left the station. You catch a bus from Lewes to Glyndebourne and there you find a theatre built in the thirties by John Christie, an opera fanatic. Tickets are very difficult to come by. The five thousand members of the Glyndebourne Festival Society have the first choice (the Society has not been taking on new members for ages) and 225 'corporate members' grab what is left. In Glyndebourne the ritual becomes decidedly abstruse. In the middle of the afternoon, under the unruffled gaze of a flock of sheep, parties and couples in full evening dress look for sheltered spots for their 'hamper and rug'.

We watched a very lively *Cosi fan tutte* with Claudio Desderi as Don Alfonso. The performance started at 5.15 pm and when after one hour and a quarter the interval came, everyone trotted back to their hampers. The old guard, enjoying the rural setting with their friends and a bottle of wine, sat on a rug or around a picnic table; the nouveaux riches, who had arrived by helicopter or in their Rolls, displayed silver candelabra, nibbled bits of lobster while they were being waited upon by their chauffeurs, turned butlers for the occasion. An hour and a quarter later they filed back in good order for the second act, a bit the worse for wear.

If Glyndebourne is the most cultural of all British summer amusements, Ascot is the most socially important, crowded and spectacular. What those two events have in common is the desperate hunting for tickets and the picnic. You go to the opera in evening dress and you eat in the park, whereas you go to the races in your morning coat and you eat in a car park. The fact that the British people have been able to convince the rest of the world that eating like that is extremely stylish, confirms my feeling that if they had applied to industry the same brilliant approach they have applied to social rituals, Great Britain would now be the Japan of Europe.

At Ascot more than anywhere else, the genuine British upper class is waging a war against the nouveaux riches: the 'real old smart' does not want to consort with 'brash new commerce', to quote the *Tatler*. The Royal Enclosure sees to that: you can only get in by personal invitation of the Queen. In the old days admission requirements were very strict, to the great delight of the socialites: divorcees were not allowed in, for instance, they had to watch from the Iron Stand just above the bookies, so it became a sort of concentration camp for marquises and duchesses who had parted company with their wives and husbands. Things have changed now: there are plenty of invitations for the Royal Enclosure and they do not cost much: £25 payable at the entrance. But they can still be difficult to get, thereby giving a sense of importance to lots of ladies in extravagant hats. Nigel Dempster, the best-known English gossip columnist, maintains that Ascot has been invaded by social climbers: he recently complained at having come face to face in the Royal Enclosure with Linda Lovelace (*Deep Throat*), 'who cannot tell one end of a horse from the other.'

Generally speaking though, at Ascot a large proportion of the people present are interested in horseracing. At Henley on the other hand, at the Royal Regatta in July, the public takes no interest in the boats and concentrates on the champagne. The Steward's Enclosure is the inner sanctum here. Rules are very strict – only in the boiling summer of 1976, were men allowed to take their jackets off – and admission is by membership. You either raced at Henley or you are hosted by someone who did. The enclosure overlooks the finishing line, so if you are interested, you can even find out who won. Not that people there worry too much about it: after a day in the sun with champagne and Pimms (41,000 bottles in one weekend) most of them cannot tell the difference between a boat and their own car.

Henley, too, is a mix of old rituals and new developments. In the enclosure, members inspect each other's clothing and reminisce on the good old days when they had no middle-age spread and could fit into a canoe. On the other side of the river, where till recently the band used to play and no one ever thought of going, scores of businesses have put up marquees and entertain clients and friends.

Finally there are the Garden Parties at Buckingham Palace. At Ascot the Queen visits, at Henley she bestows the name 'royal', but here she is the host. The guests, who are allowed to take their unmarried daughters with them, are diplomats, bishops and members of the Police, who are thus rewarded for life-long service. Waiting for an invitation to the Garden party, of which there are three a year in July, can be agonising for some. It is not any easier for foreigners but if I managed to go there twice obviously they cannot be too difficult to please these days.

Getting in trouble with a tie

'Pardon me Sir, your tie.'
'What's wrong with it?'
'Everything, Sir, if you allow me.'
'All right, go ahead. But I can't help asking myself   if ties really matter at a time like this.'
'There is no time when ties do not matter, Sir.'

                    P. G. Wodehouse, *Much Obliged, Jeeves*

The importance of clothing in people's lives is variable in Britain. Until recently it did not matter at all for the lower classes: in the North men wore drip-dry shirts and polyester suits which glowed in the dark, and women slipped their feet into blue plastic shoes more suitable for dolls which do not have to walk around Newcastle. On the other hand, gentlemen and upstarts took a fastidious interest in their clothing, feeding on literary references – Oscar Wilde must have had a quote for each item of clothing – and spending a lot of money. That has slightly altered now: at Marks & Spencer's, the department store founded in 1894 by a Polish Jew (Marks) and an Englishman (Spencer), you can now buy pure cotton underwear, pure wool jumpers and good imitation Barbour's without too much trouble.

Marks & Spencer's great success – 282 branches in Great Britain and some recent acquisitions like Brooks Brothers in the States – proves that the country has changed: British people are not only wealthier, but are prepared to spend part of their wealth to look like other Europeans. The importance of the revival has been fully grasped by the fashion industry who have found their best ambassador in the Princess of Wales. In 1987 the fashion industry's exports totalled £2 million and when Mrs Thatcher opened the London Fashion Week in 1988, she was full of praise for its contribution to the national economy.

Even the ex-Prime Minister, for whom Aquascutum used to prepare an entire wardrobe at the beginning of the year, has improved in style. When she was elected, she had some terible little hand bags and tweed suits which could have been bought by her chauffeur with his eyes shut. Now she is more sophisticated, or better advised. She even managed to be listed among the most elegant women in the world, by a very broad-minded American magazine. On public occasions she likes big hats, Gloria Swanson type, at work she opts for fully buttoned up blouses with a funny bow right under her chin. She sported a fur hat in Moscow in 1987, to the great delight of her hosts and of the photographers. She has been heard recently voicing opinions on colours and styles – 'A dark shade is a woman's best friend', 'The shoulderline dates a dress' – with the same passion and knowledge with which she discusses nuclear weapons. Carla Powell, the bubbly Italian wife of Sir Charles Powell, might be partly responsible for that. Carla knows her way around skirts, belts and shirts so it looks very likely that she was able to talk the then Prime Minister into avoiding unsuitable matches. What we know for sure is that the two women are good friends. I would like to tell you a story to prove it: true, or not, it is still funny. Carla Powell was having a very lively and gossipy telephone conversation at home, when her husband asked her to hurry up because he urgently needed to ring up the Prime Minister. 'That's all right darling,' was the answer, 'I am already talking to her.'

Every now and again, just to show that they had not yet learned their lesson in full, the above-mentioned ladies came a cropper: Diana looked like a boiled sweet and Mrs Thatcher turned up in one of those suits which would be more appropriate for her Grantham childhood friends. At an Anglo-Italian summit on Lake Maggiore, her white and brown checked dress looked more like a rustic table cloth than a prime ministerial outfit. Sarah Ferguson as well, before she became Duchess of York, had a string of mishaps: she turned up at Ascot with a horizontally striped frock; she appeared at the Chelsea Flower Show in a sort of kimono; she was seen at a polo match dressed up like Pippi Longstocking.

It is even more interesting to look at the young generation when it comes to clothing. Young British people, especially in London, say that the Europeans in general and the Italians in particular are pretty pathetic, dressing as they do, all the same way and following fashion like a flock of sheep. There must be a grain of truth in that; just look at the crowds from Milan or Rome charter flights when they land at Gatwick, all wearing the same jackets and the same shoes. Or at businessmen landing at Heathrow on regular flights and all wearing the same cashmere ties. Another Italian fad which is deemed extremely comical in England, is showing off trade marks on clothing. It might be elegant in Italy to turn up at your friends' in a jumper with Burberry's across the chest: in England they go into hysterics. It is not really in to have your initials embroidered on your shirts, but you may, if you are an estate agent with a posh car and a platinum-blond girl friend.

Fashion critics do not take only the Italians to task: on the right, traditionalists castigate bad taste, on the left the situation is a bit more complicated. 'Fashion,' writes Sarah Mower, fashion editor at the *Guardian*, 'is a moral minefield fraught with nameless dangers, vices and temptations. The seductive power of clothing affects British feelings on matters of class snobbery, puritanism, thrift, sex and justice.' In other words, do not tell friends at a party 'You look very nice tonight' (she might answer, 'Does that mean I don't normally?'), do not compliment a young writer on his shirt; either he gets angry because he thinks you are teasing him, or else he is upset because he feels silly.

Men's clothing points the way out of this minefield. Artists, journalists and academics are beyond redemption and dress exactly as they please. Visit the 'London School of Economics' and you will be able to see for yourself that there is no hope for the last group. The more famous professors are, the more shabbily they dress and they are proud of it. Otherwise an Englishman wears a uniform and seems to like the idea. In the City all you need are a pair of black shoes and a suit, it does not matter if both are old. It is better to be dressed in a scruffy two piece suit than to wear a fancy cashmere outfit. You dress as you like over the weekend: politicians give television interviews walking their dogs in the fields and wearing tattered old jumpers: no one seems to take objection. Also part of the uniform are a dinner jacket, a pair of brown shoes for the weekend and half a dozen striped shirts: in the morning the only effort required of you if you work in an office, is to choose a shirt and a tie to match. That must have beneficial psychological effects on the nation: no one can possibly be dressed better than you are at a meeting, all you might possibly see, is a different shirt. André Gide, though he was not British, saw a lot of sense in that: 'Men are more serious than women, because their clothes are darker,' he wrote.

British men are proud of the way they dress and are not open to discussion: if tradition commands that the last button on the waistcoat – vest in Savile Row – be undone, so be it. If the last button on a double breasted suit must always be done up, do not undo it. If a French businessman comes to the City in a smart St Laurent brown suit, his British counterpart will be upset. Brown, in particular, is not a popular colour for clothing: it should be used only in the country. You know the story of the Scots banker when he met his brother who had emigrated to the States and was wearing a rust-coloured suit, faced the wall and shouted in disgust 'Ginger!' Paul Keers, the author of *Classic Suits and Modern Man* tells of an old business magnate who on a similar occasion said; 'Brown looks like shit'.

Some will say that the arrogance displayed by the British when it comes to clothing shows that they still think they are the masters of the world. It would be unfair to say that: in truth Great Britain is perfectly entitled to set the rules. The 'classic style' in clothing which has not changed much, became widespread during the Industrial Revolution when men gave up their dandy outfits and adopted the sober look immortalised by the Victorian gentleman. The Duke of Windsor brought it to perfection and became its paragon. He set the rules during his foreign visits between 1930 and 1937 and imposed fads and fashions still popular nowadays, like the Windsor knot or the chalkstripe.

As we cannot set out all the rules for all the different items of clothing nor go into all the details, we shall only talk of suits, shirts and ties. Suits must be dark and look worn – Beau Brummel had his worn first by a valet – they must have two side pockets (a third one may be added on casual wear) and two buttons at the front. There were three of them at the beginning of the century and one only in the sixties: in Savile Row, tailors put two buttons on, but traditionalists insist on three. As for the buttons on the jacket sleeves – which were introduced by Napoleon to stop his soldiers wiping their noses on them – there must be four and they must be real buttons with real buttonholes. In the old days sleeves could be turned up if need be, nowadays they are the hallmark of the bespoken suit and the buttons must never be undone for any reason. In his *Fall of the Public Man* Richard Sennet wrote, 'It is always possible to recognise a gentleman because the buttons on his jacket sleeve can be undone and done up again. You can recognise the real gentleman because his buttons are always done up, so that your attention is not drawn to that detail.'

Shirts are an equally strange business. For £30 to £50, you can find in any shop in Jermyn Street those enormous shirts with bold vertical stripes which came into fashion in 1870, when shirts with buttons all the way down came on to the market (they used to be put on head first until then). They were not immediately popular, nicknamed 'regatta shirts', and were not deemed acceptable in an office, partly because it was thought that the stripes were there to hide the grime on collars and cuffs. A compromise was reached: collars and cuffs had to be white regardless of the colour of the shirt (these are still fashionable: the former Liberal leader Sir David Steel is very fond of them, though they seem to make him look even more like a school boy). Not all the 85 million shirts sold every year in Great Britain – 3.6 per male – are pure cotton: only 30 per cent of them are, while the 'cotton rich' variety, in which there is more cotton than artificial fibre, is gaining ground. According to a survey conducted at Harvie & Hudson, the most popular shirt is the 'blue and white Bengal stripe', in which the stripes, both blue and white, are exactly one eighth of an inch wide. We simply call them blue striped shirts.

There are rules for shirts as well, to the great delight of those in the know and also to enable the ancient shop assistants in Jermyn Street to size you up at a glance. They are quite extraordinary people there: in the dimly lit shop, every order for a made to measure shirt is entered in a battered old book which is entrusted to an assistant in tails. Americans are spellbound and come all the way across the Atlantic to watch the ritual; if they knew that at the back of the shop accountants are at work with their computers, they would have a fit. A good shirt – they will explain to you if you can understand them – depends on the following details: the collar must be made of two layers of material, the back seam in two halves (originally to fit each shoulder, one at a time), no breast pockets, enough material at the back to match the front of the shirt in between the legs. Collars can be cutaways to accomodate a Windsor knot, or the traditional turndowns. The button-downs were invented for polo players to stop collars flapping during the game, and are very popular with Americans. Cuffs can have either a single button or, in the more casual wear, two. Cuff-links are very formal and so is the gauntlet cuff.

We come now to ties, which is normally where foreigners get into problems. British ties must be bought carefully and worn even more carefully, because unlike French and Italian ones, they always have a meaning. Let me explain: if you walk into the Tie Rack in Kensington High Street and buy a spotted tie for £3.95, you only run the risk of buying a mediocre tie (if it twists when you hold it from the narrow end, the cut is not across the weave). If you wear a tie with little hippopotami on a dark background in Milan, it does not mean very much, but in London it means that you are a member of the legendary Leander Rowing Club founded in 1820 and you run the risk of being seriously embarrassed when you come nose to nose with a real member in a restaurant.

Even more dangerous are the ties associated with the traditonal British networks: a regiment, an association, a public school, or worse a particular group or team in a public school. What happened to Lord Tonypandy is an often quoted example. In the fifties when he was not yet Lord Tonypandy, but simply George Thomas the new MP for Cardiff Central, he decided to buy a beautiful black tie with a narrow blue diagonal stripe for his very first appearance in the Commons. As he walked in, there was such an uproar from the Tory benches that the Tory whip, Captain Chichester-Clark, had to grab him and take him out. 'My dear sir,' he said, 'do you realise that you are wearing an Old Etonian tie?' The young man was petrified; eventually he managed to explain that he had bought the tie at a sale in his hometown.

If it is any consolation to foreigners, even British people have problems in finding their way around in this minefield. For a start there are over ten thousand meaningful patterns currently in use (according to P. L. Sell & Co, the largest British manufacturer). Some patterns are the same: a member of the Second Indian Grenadiers could be mixed up with a Westminster Hospital Old Boy. Others think that it is a trifle vulgar and lacking self-assurance to wear a tie in order to manifest what group you belong to. Finally the unanswered question: where do you wear an old school tie? There is a story about a young Etonian who was strolling in his club wearing his old school tie, when he was rebuked by an old member slumped in an armchair: 'I do not think you should wear an Old Etonian tie in town'. To which the young man replied: 'But sir, I am about to go off to the country.' Unmoved the old gentleman retorted: 'I always thought you put the tie on at Chiswick roundabout.'

8

Vices

British bad habits are many and varied and British people know each and everyone of them. Sometimes during a party and with the help of a bottle of wine to overcome their embarrassment, the national disease, the British themselves list them for the benefit of the foreigners around the table. And here is the first bad habit, but not the worst: they drink far more than they should. British people spend a daily £35 million, one fifth of their shopping bill, on alcohol. At any party, celebration, gathering, ceremony or christening you find yourself with a glass in your hand before even taking your coat off. The fear of alcohol which the Protestant Church preached for centuries goes hand in hand with a passionate interest in the subject: the British wax lyrical when they describe the warmth and friendship in a pub just before closing time and they are almost sincere after the fourth gin and tonic.

The trouble is that unlike the French and Italians, they drink to get drunk. In many parts of England and almost everywhere in Scotland and Wales, getting drunk with your friends is part of Saturday night and two bottles of wine for a dinner party of six is simply not enough. When they want to meet someone the British say: 'Let's have a drink some-time', thereby implying that a full glass is an integral part of their social life. Some groups and professions seem particularly busy destroying their livers: British journalists, for instance, pop out for a pint as frequently as their counterparts in Milan or Rome have a coffee: as a result the former have a reputation for being drunkards and the latter for being neurotic.

When it comes to drinks anything goes and of late the British have parted company with tradition. Forty years ago beer represented 82 per cent of all sales of alcohol; now it is down to 55 per cent. Lager is much more popular than real ale and is behind all the layers of fat bulging out of tee shirts and belts in the summer. Wine is coming on very fast: in 1950 it was 4.7 per cent of the market, now it is 20 per cent and is a very popular talking point, especially amongst people who know nothing about it. The British continue to drink sherry and port, about which they know everything and champagne about which they pretend to know something. The choice of drink goes hand in hand with class divisions: the working classes love beer, the upper classes like French wines, the middle classes drink both and keep quiet about it.

Much to their credit, the British themselves are perfectly aware of their vices. For instance, they acknowledge that they are fascinated by the mix of politics and sex (more so if it is prostitution and particularly if it is homosexuality); they like spies and crimes, though they are upset by them; they love gambling and good food, after having eaten badly for generations. And they cannot make up their minds about Europe: some find it too exotic, some exhausting. But they are not beyond redemption, as foreigners tend to think when making hasty judgements on their first visit to Britain. Leaving aside hooligans and the like, I think I agree with what Samuel Butler said in *The Way of All Flesh*: 'Half the vices the world most vehemently condemns have the seed of goodness in them and must be practised in moderation rather than aiming at total abstinence.' The son of a clergyman, he was a strange person. He went to Cambridge and ended up in New Zealand to farm sheep. The book appeared after his death in 1903, because he did not have the courage to publish it while he was still alive. Come to think of it, hypocrisy is a very British habit.

All Right, Let's Eat

British people eat worse than they would like to, but much better than we think they do. Italian teenagers flying in from Milan and Turin start complaining as soon as they land and carry on for the whole length of their stay. Above all they cannot stand boiled vegetables, strange meat pies and roast lamb: its not clear whether they make a big deal of it to deflect attention from what they have been up to with the Scandinavian teenagers on the same course, or whether their grievances are genuine.

The British did suffer though for years and in silence. In 1967 David Frost and Anthony Jay said something very true, namely that British people have always made correlations between virtue and diet. Boarding schools' atrocious food had produced bright strong lads capable of winning battles and glory for the nation. But haute cuisine, like other optionals such as sex and bidets, had a bad effect on foreigners: it had to be avoided at all costs. Better to eat tough meat, mysterious pies and soggy vegetables, if they had made Britain great. Only Royalty were allowed to eat well and they did so, as shown by Edward VII's stomach. (It was not an accident that he was a francophile.) For generations overfed babies have been looked upon with disapproval, sauces raised suspicions and the three great Quaker families who set up British confectionery – Rowntree, Cadbury and Fry – felt so guilty about it, that they gave large chunks of their profits away to charity.

Things changed in the fifties at the end of rationing when Chinese and Greek restaurants appeared and Italian cafés increased in number. Whatever pride the British were taking in their cooking has been destroyed by the advent of fast food: it has been said that when you order a superburger and a king-size milk shake, you lose your self-respect for ever.

American food has had an enormous impact; Wimpy,

McDonald's and Kentucky Fried Chicken have a £3.5 billion turnover, but they have remained quite separate from the traditional diet. Not even in the outskirts of Newcastle will you find people having a cheeseburger for Sunday lunch. French cooking on the other hand has crept into the British way of life and has taken over the cookery pages in weekly magazines. So housewives are being taught about soufflés and there are more and more 'Anglo-French' restaurants where young chefs cross nouvelle cuisine with traditional British cooking with varying results and a regular enthusiastic public response. A number of Italian, Greek and Spanish dishes are part of the daily diet of millions of people, except for a few alterations: the majority of the British cannot yet understand why spaghetti is a first course in Italy. Obviously when you have struggled for half an hour with your fork, you have no energy left. George Mikes imagined this dialogue between a Yorkshire miner and his wife: 'What is that, Doris, paella? Paella again? All right I like paella, but paella every day, bloody paella and nothing else! Why can't I have a good old decent ratatouille for a change?'

The love of cooking – the desire to eat decently, some would say – has had spin-offs in other directions. For a start the number of customers who return their steak tartare because it is underdone is going down regularly, and newspapers like *The Times* have been writing long lyrical articles about restaurants (take this assessment of a place in Fulham Road which was nominated 'Italian restaurant of the year 1987': 'The risotto is pure ambrosia, it is unbeliveable, such delicious risotto should be known under another name.') Harrods' food halls have become a temple, where after buying a quarter of gammon, people wander in ecstatsy for hours and not only because they cannot find the way out. The food in the smarter supermarkets has improved dramatically. The food department of Marks & Spencer – a chain once famous solely for its underwear – is now spoken of with wonder. As for Sainsbury's, which almost exclusively sells food, people talk about it with grateful tears in their eyes. There are now also an increasing number of television programmes where short, plump middle-aged men with a French accent, talk for half an hour about the sauce they are preparing. For some British people 'eating out' is their only social activity. Apart from ethnic restaurants where Greeks stick to their kebabs and Indians to curry, menus tend to follow the current fashion. The present one is fish, which is selling in ever increasing quantities. Things like monkfish and mackerel, which used to be fed to the cat, are now the subject of learned discussions among experts. Melanie Davis, who produced a programme about *haute cuisine* on Yorkshire Television at the end of 1989, summed it up very neatly: 'We used to eat full stop. Now we actually look at what is on the plate.'

But do not be fooled. The traditional British food, the sort that encourages Italians to spend their holidays somewhere else, is still around. And so it should be, since many eating habits are deeply rooted. Suet puddings remind British people of their school days; roast lamb and mint sauce, bring back memories of Sunday lunches, the only pleasant moment in the otherwise dreary day, and crumpets are an indulgence (but one quickly grows tired of having hands and everything else covered in melted butter). Strawberries and cream represent Wimbledon even to those who never managed to get there. Cold roast beef and Stilton – a hard blue veined cheese which Daniel Defoe used to eat with a spoon, maggots and all – reminds one of snatched lunches at the pub. Only breakfast has gone down the drain. Working mothers discovered sometime ago that they had no time to prepare eggs, bacon, porridge, toast, mushrooms, tomatoes and so on in the morning. Wealthy families who liked a steaming, piping hot breakfast, when staff made it, are not prepared to get up on dark winter mornings in a cold house.

Unfortunately for them, the working classes carry on with their sausages, chips and baked beans, the trio which is almost like the Union Jack. The consequences are appalling for their livers and their hearts. Not long ago two dieticians of the British Society for Nutritional Medicine reported the following discovery: teenagers brought up on junk food, such as the above plus chocolate and icecream, are potential hooligans since their brains do not work properly. This theory is backed not only by the smell you come across at football stadia, but by evidence supplied by Ian Jack, a journalist who has worked for both the *Observer* and the *Sunday Times*. In the wake of the Heysel stadium tragedy, he went to Turin. He wanted to compare the two cities and came back with the firm belief that the British working classes had a lot to learn from Italians, especially about food. 'I went to the home of Mr Domenico Lopreiato who works at FIAT and lives in the outskirts of Turin,' he said. 'Mrs Lopreiato told me that she only bought fresh food, apart from tinned tuna. She makes her own pasta sauce – tomatoes, olive oil, salt and basil – has her wine sent up from Calabria, which we tasted over a lunch of pasta, veal cutlets, salad, four sorts of cheese, and fresh fruits.' In Liverpool, blue-collar workers shop at Kwik-Save: bread, potatoes, eggs, baked beans. In places like Toxteth, teenage mothers take greasy bags of chips home to their three-year-olds, who will eat them cold with ketchup.

Sex and the toothpaste tube

When Henry Kissinger said 'Power is the ultimate aphrodisiac', he was certainly thinking of the British. For some time now it seems that Ministers, MP's and Party Chairmen have been regularly involved in sex scandals, either with their secretaries, or with dancers, or policemen or masseuses. Why has this sort of scandal become part of British life even more than Wimbledon?

To find an answer to that question, it is useful to make a quick recap of the past twenty-five years. The only scandal which did not involve a Tory, the Conservatives proudly point out, was the homosexual one, (Thorpe, Liberal, 1979).

There are plenty of theories about this Tory monopoly. Gordon Newman, who wrote a play (*The Honorable Trade*) on the subject, says that the two reasons why Tories have the most sex scandals are the following: first, as they all went to boarding school, they left home at a young age and are therefore in need of affection and want to be loved. The second reason is their party ideology. 'Conservatives' says Mr Newman, 'are in favour of free enterprise: sex is not much different: when you see your chance, grab it.'

Hugh Montgomery Hyde, the author of *An Intricate Web: Sex scandals in politics and in British society*', maintains that one should look at British past history. Lord Melbourne, Prime Minister in the last century, loved being whipped. Lord Castlereagh used to visit the prostitutes in St James's Park on his way home from the Commons. The last young lady turned out to be a young boy and Lord Castlereagh, overwhelmed with shame, took his own life. Lord Palmerston attempted rape on one of the ladies attending Queen Victoria at Windsor Castle: he was acquitted because he could prove that he had entered the wrong room and that there was indeed a lady waiting for him.

Modern scandals, which the British remember with affection, began in 1960. The first one was about Christine Keeler, the girl for whom a Tory Minister lost his head, his face and his job in that order. The story exploded in 1963: at the time Miss Keeler was nineteen, she wore banana leaves – when she was wearing anything at all – and had in her bed either the British War Secretary (Profumo) or Captain Evgenij Ivanov, a military attaché at the Soviet Embassy. Today people still remember the story with nostalgia and like to talk about it: in March 1989 when a film called *Scandal* based on Miss Keeler's recollections was being discussed, lords and Anglican bishops also contributed to the debates.

As a result of the Profumo affair the fall of Harold Macmillan's government was hastened, the sexual revolution in Britain got under way and the two girls at the centre of it became living legends. Christine Keeler, now forty-five, does now look her age, whereas Mandy Rice-Davies is still blonde, bubbly and sexy. She recently published a thriller entitled *Today and Tomorrow* about – surprise, surprise – the liaison between a politician and a prostitute.

There followed a succession of scandals to be drooled over by the British – mostly simple affairs to do with extra-marital sex – occasionally with more sinister overtones. The key players are frequently exonerated, but it doesn't seem to stop the press from having their day.

If one had to pick a single example that best illustrates the British obsession with politicians' often frankly mundane sex lives, then surely it would be the Parkinson affair of 1983. Cecil Parkinson was then Industry Secretary, having been Chairman of the Conservative Party and a member of the inner cabinet during the Falklands war and was tipped as a possible successor to Mrs Thatcher. Mr Parkinson committed political suicide in the easiest way (he subsequently made a come back): he knocked up his secretary, Sarah Keyes, promised to divorce his wife to marry her, then changed his mind. The young woman was ever so disappointed: she spilled the beans to a couple of *Times* journalists and dictated an article with the headline, 'I begged him to tell Mrs Thatcher'. On resigning, Mr Parkinson, made the following comment, the deeper meaning of which was not fully grasped by most people at the time: 'It's no use: you cannot put the toothpaste back into the tube.'

Before closing this section, I would like to dwell on the exploits of Mrs Cynthia Payne, 55, a truly national character, who inspired books, plays and successful films. She became a household name in 1979 when fifty-three people, including a lord, an Irish MP and various Anglican Church dignitaries, were found in her house in Ambleside Avenue in Streatham, in the company of a crowd of young prostitutes. One of the clients, a man aged seventy, told the Police: 'I thought it was a Christmas Party.' All of them had paid with luncheon vouchers: that way the madam thought she would not get in trouble with the law. She was obviously wrong because she was locked up for eighteen months.

Mrs Payne was in court again recently. The charges against her were very much the same as in the good old days. Sixty people had been caught redhanded in her Ambleside Avenue home. Most were between fifty and sixty. Most were busy with young prostitutes. Five of them were dressed in women's clothes, one as a French maid. According to the very detailed police report, which was submitted to the jury complete with pictures, things were going on all over the place: on the landings, in every room and in every bathroom. A young lady, says the report, 'apparently surprised by the Police entrance, jumped up and as a result one of the guests rolled into the bathtub.' A witness, Miss Jana Lynn, a thirty-seven-year-old with a strange Scandinavian accent, explained giggling to the court that she 'would have sex and possibly something else for £25' but vigorously denied 'having had more than three men in her room in one evening'. The trial, which I attended, was, according to the British press, one of the most exhilarating affairs of the century. In the end Mrs Payne was acquitted and to celebrate she organised an intimate party in a suite in a smart hotel in Park Lane. The management asked her never to go there again.

Of dogs and yuppies

All one understands on entering Wembley stadium for the first-time on a Friday evening to go to the races, is that greyhounds are smaller than horses. After that the event is fascinating to watch, but impossible to understand. The greyhounds run exceedingly fast – 'they would not be here, if they didn't' exclaims a local, surprised by our surprise – and each race is over on average in thirty seconds. Which is just enough time to understand which one is number 4, the one with the black coat, and to guess that somebody else has won the race. The programme, intended to help me to place my bet, was like double Dutch to me. This is what it said about Liverpool Wonder (I think one should bet on it on the strength of the name): Oct 28 490 6 5.91 4335 5 6 Aubawn Cutler BCrd 30.24+10 25.8 3/1 A6 30.82 Season 9.6.87. After having been informed that the last figure refers to when Liverpool Wonder was last on heat, I gave up over the rest.

Greyhound racing, a sport which till recently belonged to the urban working class, is now changing its following. You can see 'at the dogs' more and more well to do young men, conspicuous by their clothing – smart casual is a plague in London as well as in Milan – and for the silly questions they ask. First, when a few thirty-year-olds came along with their girl friends, the press reported the phenomenon which prompted more thirty-year-olds to bring their girl friends too. Considering the variety of new activities the young rich have been trying out in London, an evening at the dogs looks like a sensible choice: it is cheap (entrance £2), it is very lively, quite unusual and if you are enterprising enough you can pull a bird: British working-class girls may not wear any stockings at any time of the year, but they are healthy and broadminded.

So thanks to the yuppies and the press, the greyhound industry is back in full swing after falling on very hard times (culminating in the conversion of White City [west London] into a carpark). Today the races are held at Wembley in the stadium itself – footballers run up and down, whereas greyhounds run round and round – and at Wimbledon, Walthamstow and Catford (the last two locations are in the south-east of London). There are four restaurants at Walthamstow, where surrounded by glittering neon decor, waitresses dressed up like Barbarella serve four thousand meals every Saturday night. Anyway, there are three meetings a week at Wembley – Monday, Wednesday and Friday – with an audience of about 1,600 people. There are lots of young couples: the blokes with Ford Sierras and dressed like drug pushers, the girls in miniskirts and betting only on greyhounds with interesting names. There is another place at Hackney where only the working classes go. There, a lonely seventy-three-year-old woman works behind the desk: she has a wooden leg, I am informed by someone who has taken the trouble to check.

I advise you to go to Wembley if you wish to go to the races. There you can see a mix of old aficionados and new fans under the benevolent gaze of the bookies dressed in fur coats. The stadium is being renovated: a new stand is being built under the Grandstand Restaurant, so the scaffolding hides the ring. To get over the problem, the management has installed closed circuit television. So you see old couples, their eyes riveted on the screens, forgetting to eat – honestly they don't miss much – and then diligently writing down both results and odds on their programmes with a biro. A shoal of waiters weaves around the tables: they serve beer and a very light pink smoked salmon (not included on the table d'hôte menu), while girls collect the bets. Newcomers prefer to go to the bookies themselves, the waiters cannot stand them because they get in the way, but they have learned to wriggle past them while serving the beer and salmon.

The restaurant can seat about a hundred people. The rest are downstairs around the bookies. There are twelve races in an evening, fifteen minutes apart. People who cannot face the bookmakers' icy gaze rely on the tote: you can place your bet on the winner, on the place and on a series of mysterious combinations (Forecast, Each Way, Trio, Straight Line and Reversed). The minimum stake is 50 pence. City people who are familiar with figures learn quickly. Foreigners have problems with the language, get on everyone's nerves and walk around with a weak smile on their faces looking blank.

Among the public, many people are familiar with the greyhounds and their extravagant names (Decoy Madonna/ Who's Sorry Now – Full Whisper/Ring Rhapsody/Corrigeen Time – Gone West/Easy My Son). The owners are strange, romantic people more in love with the dogs than with their wives. They spend Sundays walking them in the fields and rarely make much money. The prize money for each race is about £100 and is put up by the bookies: they make the money, just look at their huge cars and at their flashy women. The only hound that turned out a real money-spinner was Ballyreagan Bob: in 1985 he won a record thirty-two times in a row. A rather placid animal, he used to set of slowly and when he looked hopelessly left behind, would catch up as if propelled by an engine. In any British pub the sheer mention of Ballyreagan Bob can still move people to tears.

Not even the yuppies and their partners have changed the status of greyhound racing: riding is the sport of kings, greyhounds the pleasure of the working man. They themselves assure me that they would far rather spend an evening at Catford than an afternoon at Ascot. Hounds are after all no less aristocratic animals than horses and besides they do not have jockeys on their backs who can forget to win. Hounds are mentioned in Shakespeare and Chaucer. The Abbess of Sopwell in her *Boke of St Albans* (1486) praised the hound which was 'headed lyke a snake, an neckeyed lyke a drake, backed lyke a beam, syded lyke a bream, footed lyke a cattle, tallyd lyke a rat'. Here is a plainer description of the fine relationship between these animals and the working classes: 'Keep off shorts and horses, stick to pints and dogs.' That is what fathers told their sons in the days when both dressed like Andy Capp, Britain smelled of coal, and dogs and yuppies kept well apart.

Let's go abroad

I suspected for a long time that the British tourist was a particular breed. I confirmed my fears were when I found the following dialogue in *The Genleman's Pocket Companion*, a booklet of useful phrases for the English gentleman abroad 1781.

ITALIAN MAID: 'Does Sir need anything else?'

ENGLISH GENTLEMAN: 'Yes, my dear, snuff the candle and come close to me. Give me a kiss, so I can sleep better.'

ITALIAN MAID: 'But how can you be ill if you talk about kissing! I'd sooner die than kiss a man in his bed or any-where else. May the Lord grant you a peaceful night and a good rest.'

ENGLISH GENTLEMAN: 'Thank you very much, my good woman.'

It was at the time of the Grand Tour that the British tourist dreamt of engaging in such conversation. After 1763, at the end of the Seven Years' War against France, when British relationships with the Catholic States improved, the upper classes used their recent wealth from the Industrial Revolution to travel extensively. And the Grand Tour was considered the finishing touch to a liberal education. It altered the prevailing taste in painting and architecture, gave birth to great romantic fantasies, a passionate love of antiquities, boundless enthusiasm for sun, wine, food and young girls. For the above reason Adam Smith considered the Grand Tour a pernicious institution as 'young people come back ever more debauched, conceited, useless and unprincipled. Nothing apart from the sad state of British Universities, can possibly give a good name to such an absurd practice as travelling.' No one listened to him. All the Men of Discretion went south looking for Knowledge and Truth. If they found a maid or a young lad as well, so much the better.

Two hundred years later the British are still at it. And not just that: besides going to Spain, indeed flying anywhere there is any sun, they enjoy reading about their predecessors' travels. Two books have recently been published on the topic: *The Grand Tour* by Christopher Hibbert and *The Mediterranean Passion* by John Pemble. The latter takes a very close look at the reasons why in Victorian times British people came to Italy. For a start they did not come in July or August and like any good tourist, they looked for places without tourists. They dreaded 'the burning rays of the sun which turn the sand into a blazing desert' as much as 'the languor of the Southern tribes' (John Ruskin). They drew hasty conclusions about economic backwardness, superstition, climate and religion, and most of all they felt vastly superior. 'If we had no other reason for being pleased about being Protestant, it would be sufficient to consider that our religion prevents us from being as ridiculous as the people here,' wrote the Reverend Henry Christmas. According to Mr Pemble, the reason why at the end of the last century ninety thousand Britons came to Italy every year is one or more of the following: pilgrimage, culture, health, gambling, or homosexuality. He draws the following conclusion: if the visits by Victorian tourists did not add much to the knowledge of the Mediterranean, they added a lot to the knowledge of the tourists themselves.

As there are no scientific studies about the current English migrations, we have to rely on hard facts and figures.

Eight million people – 70 per cent of those who go on package holidays – go to Spain, where they lose their inhibitions. The media back home give a running account of what they get up to, but they are resigned to it: people go to France for the wine, to Greece for the suntan and to Spain for a brawl. When the early birds leave on the first charter flights from Gatwick in June, the Sunday supplements remind the nation of the goings on in Benidorm on the Costa del Sol; tabloids chip in with accounts of drunken behaviour and fights, while the rest of the press turns the spotlight on Manchester typists' steamy nights and leaves you with the impression that as soon as a British girl finds herself in good company in her swimming costume, she cannot wait to take it off.

A week in Spain booked at the last moment can cost as little as £99. Those who go with wife, children and factor 15 suncream usually only want to get away from another miserable British summer and are perfectly happy to cook in the sun while sipping a long drink. A small number of youngsters – occasionally tattooed, regularly drunk, called 'the animals' in Torremolinos – prefer fights, possibly with the locals. Every Police station on the coast has its story to tell. Every year there are more arrests and casualties and every now and again a few fatalities: in 1988 a taxi driver died of a heart attack after being set upon by a gang of them.

These are the people who are called hooligans when they come in the wake of a football team: we know full well what they are capable of. In the spring of 1985, right after the Heysel tragedy, I was in Liverpool. I saw them cry in their club's flags while still wearing on their faces the marks of their excesses; but that was only a very rare example of collective remorse after a very big mess. In the European Championships of 1988 in Germany there was only the mess. 'We attacked the Dutch because we thought they were better hooligans than we are,' one of them explained very seriously after the fight near Düsseldorf Station. Another so-called fan who was expelled even before the beginning of the matches boasted on the ferry back home: 'I am Europe's top thug.' It is quite likely that when he arrived at Dover and saw 'World War Three!' splashed across the front pages of the tabloids, he was flattered.

Only 800,000 British tourists go to Italy every year and they are very different from those who go to German stadia or to Spanish beaches. As in their opinion it is slightly lower class to have a good time together, this more sophisticated lot, who love Venice, Rome and Tuscany, ignore their fellow nationals who come to visit Venice, Rome and Tuscany. They are a bit upset when they meet each other in the trattorias they thought they had discovered. Highly strung, they come along with all their sensibilities: only after a couple of strikes and a mugging do they agree with the English author of the beginning of the century who said that 'the Italians were the only black spot in a magic land'. But as soon as they cross the Alps heading back north, they are reconciled with Samuel Johnson's 'A man who has not been in Italy, is always conscious of an inferiority', and they use the quote later on in the autumn at dinner parties with friends who preferred Kent to Chianti.

When it comes to France, British people love mainly Brittany and Provence, the former because it is near home, the latter because of the sound of the name. Switzerland is popular in the winter and not just because Mrs Thatcher goes there in the summer: no upper-class thirty-year-old will go without his week in the chalet during which he skis very little, drinks a lot and does not learn that the 't' in chalet must not be sounded. There are hundreds of charter flights to Greece and Turkey – the latter is very popular these days – for very plain young people who are only after clean water and cheap restaurants. If anyone ever wanted to write a book about them, his inspiration would dry up after a few pages.

Twenty million Britons, with a lot of misplaced trust in the British climate, choose the local beaches. If they chose them for their ingrained melancholy, their crumbling piers, their Indian cupolas, or for thoughtfully walking on the pebbles by the seashore, they would come home contented. But they are looking for sea and sunshine, so they come back dissatisfied. Even the word 'holidaymaker' sounds like a warning: you are making your holidays. The American equivalent, 'vacationer', sounds more promising. But Americans would not stay on very long in places like Bognor Regis or Skegness, unless you tied them up very tight.

9

Virtues

Don't worry, it is still all English

Great Britain is greatly amused by the summit meetings of French-speaking countries, by the cries of pain of the Académie Française and by the French attempts to get rid of 'le weekend', 'le ferry boat', 'le duty free', in favour of 'la fin de semaine', 'le navire transbordeur', 'la boutique franche'. The British maintain that their language needs no academies, no summit meetings, no manifestoes for the very simple reason that it was already won the battle. English is the most widely used language in 101 out of 171 countries in the world; three out of four business letters, three television broadcasts out of five, half the scientific papers and magazines, 80 per cent of computer data, are in English. Streets and piazzas all over the planet are full of Art-Shops, Multicleans, Drive-ins, Hamburger Restaurants, Flash Copy's and Fitness Centres.

The British say that the great success of the English language is due to three things, two of which are pretty obvious, and a third one which is not so evident. For a start grammar and syntax are extremely simplified, at least in the basic language; and secondly, British colonial expansion was followed by American economic success, when the former came to an end the latter took over. The third reason is the great flexibility of the language. In Great Britain there is no 'language protectionism' of any sort: if other nations want to take the English language and make a mess of it, they are free to do so.

There are countless examples of the adaptability of the English language to other customs and to other requirements. The Japanese have turned 'mass communications' into 'masukomi' while 'nonsense' has become 'nansensu'. 'See how the great democratic institutions are developing here in India' sounds like 'Dekho great democratic kaise India main develop ho rahy hain' in Hindi. In Nigeria 'biscuits' becomes 'biskit' in Hausa.

The English the Australians and the New Zealanders use, is another example of how the language can be distorted without the British getting worked up about it – we shall talk later about American/English. Down under, for example, a 'motorcyclist' is a 'bickie' (short for motorbike), a 'lorry driver' becomes a 'truckie' (from the American 'truck'). Rupert Murdoch, the Australian proprietor of *The Times*, imported 'journos' for 'journalists' into Great Britain. This last term, which came into use at the time of the Wapping dispute, was not very popular to start with but now it is quite commonplace because it is so short.

Philip Howard, literary editor at *The Times*, is one of many who think that 'pure English', the equivalent of Hochdeutsch or of the Italian spoken in Florence, does not exist any longer. Fifty years ago that language was taught in public schools and was spoken in south-east England. Thirty years ago, BBC announcers read the nine o'clock news in their dinner jackets and spoke in BBC English, which meant that they had all the mannerisms and the accents of the upper middle class (their pronunciation was far too good for the real upper class). In the sixties the language followed the general trend: the first announcers with an unmistakable, lower-middle-class accent appeared on BBC: they said 'Ufrica' when they meant Africa and proudly showed off their regional accents (now it is the same on commercial television, the den of virile female journalists from Manchester). The BBC has been tightening the reins recently but otherwise the upper class keeps mumbling, the upper middle class keeps imitating it; and anything goes when it comes to accents: as long as you are successful and have plenty of money, there are no problems in being asked to dinner parties.

In spite of all that, the British still have to choose their words very carefully and as for foreigners, they find life very difficult and end up getting it wrong every single time, but they are forgiven. Accent and vocabulary are, as a matter of fact, a powerful indicator of social origin, though the polls say that half the British think they have no accent, while the other half would be prepared to swear that it is not true at all, of course.

Here are some examples: loo, bathroom, gents, ladies, lavatory, toilet, convenience, lav, water-closet, WC, bog, john, can, heads, latrines, privy, little girl's room, powder room, khasi are all words for the same thing. In fact 'loo', used to be upper class, but since the upper middle class has been using it, the upper class has gone back to lavatory. The lower middle classes, trying to sound elegant and to show off their French, prefer 'toilet' as well as pardon, serviette, perfume and gateau, to everyone else's horror.

Things are not as clear as that all the time. The upper class and the lower class talk of pudding, while the middle class says dessert. Your plumber can turn up on your doorstep and say 'How do you do?' just as a duke would, but a young intellectual might easily say 'How are you doing?' 'Mirror' though has won the battle against the more elegant 'looking glass' and as for radio, only a handful of upper-class show-offs, will insist on 'wireless'. The Sloane Rangers not only gave Princess Di to the world but also a particular language full of actuallys, awfullys and reallys. The young fogeys, the latest of the young tribes, do not say 'hi' but 'hallo', not 'see you' but 'so long', and never 'have a nice day'.

Let's forget accents and carry on praising the English language. It is so vigorous that it has absorbed, without any apparent problems, a number of foreign words such as kindergarten from German, chauffeur from French, cookie from Dutch where it means little cake, and it has increased its vocabulary enormously with technical terms, Americanisms, and words from former colonies; 'tandoori' for example, which is an Indian cookery term from the word 'tandoor' – oven in Urdu. Today the English language has the largest vocabulary in the world: half a million words and three hundred thousand technical terms. The British take their revenge on this reverse colonisation by treating all linguistic imports with arrogance. Even place names get into trouble: try to ask for Beauchamp Place ('Beecham' to English speakers) with the correct French pronunciation, no taxi driver will understand you and every one will accuse you of showing off.

The problem with a rapidly evolving language is that words and expressions go out of fashion and out of use. Or more accurately they are still used by Italian English teachers who come over to London relying on their 1967 vocabulary, when they visited Britain in their student days. Things like 'groovy' which was trendy at the time of the Beatles are now antiques (for some reason it is still in use in Northern Ireland but it means 'terribly ugly'). The same has happened to 'smashing,' 'magic,' 'fabulous', 'epic', 'brilliant': now they say 'brill', but linguists are sure that that will not last long because of its very ugliness. The British themselves have problems occasionally: Patricia Wheatly, who works at the BBC, told us that she had difficulties in understanding two people she was talking to. One was a forty-year-old producer who was using the terminology of the swinging sixties (things like 'let's cool it', or 'let's split'), while a nineteen-year-old secretary had come up with 'It's my crack', a brand new imported expression.

When it comes to language, fashions come and go very quickly. Among the 'typical expressions of the eighties' which Oliver Pritchett collected for the *Sunday Telegraph* there is 'inner city' which was first used at the time of the race riots in Birmingham and Liverpool. When further troubles exploded in districts like Brixton and Tottenham, which are not in the centre of London, but in suburbia, they were still called 'inner city riots'. Other expressions have been imposed by the media and by very unimaginative journalists: things like 'enterprise economy' to make it sound American, or 'rescue package' (of which Westland had a fair collection), or 'urban deprivation', always to be found with 'inner city', and of course 'disaffected youth'. Prince Charles for his part, finds an answer in 'community architecture' (why not ask him what he means?).

The turbulent transformation of the language has resulted in very big mistakes, a widespread practice which upsets the five writers who publish in the *Spectator* and does not bother the remaining fifty-six million Britons at all. *The Economist*, one of the best British weeklies, has even prepared a handbook full of good advice intended for its own journalists. I read in it that an 'alternative' is between two and not three or more things; that you say 'circumstances in which' and not 'under which'; that 'come up with' means to suggest and is better than 'suggest' itself; that 'to compare with' underlines differences, and 'to compare to' draws attention to similarities, as in 'Shall I compare thee to a summer's day?' I also see that 'different' goes with 'from' not with 'to' or 'than'; 'effectively' means 'having an effect' and not 'actually'; 'presently' stands for 'in a short while' and not 'now'. 'The reason that' is the correct form for 'the reason why' (in spite of Lord Tennyson's poem), and finally an agreement is in any case 'verbal' and if it is not written, it is 'oral'.

Besides mistakes there are also loads of Americanisms in the English language as spoken by the British themselves. 'Additional' (and), 'corporation' (company), 'neighbourhood' (district), 'regular' (ordinary), 'meet with' (meet), 'riders' (passengers) are but a few. The strong transatlantic influence is also responsible for all the troubles with the use of the past tenses.

A good example of linguistic pollution, that is the ability of the English language to worm its way into another language, is the Italian spoken by Italian expats in Great Britain. They end up talking badly and writing no better. I found all sorts of things from 'eventualmente' (which means 'perhaps' in Italian) used for 'eventually', to a confusion between 'attitudine' and 'attitude' (the former is the Italian for 'aptitude'). This attrocious practice is in daily use in London's Italian restaurants where you are served 'vegetali' (in proper Italian 'legumi') and in books, magazines and everywhere in the Italian press where 'monumento' has become 'memoriale' (straight from 'memorial').

God save 'The Firm', the Queen can look after herself

In Great Britain republicans are fewer in number than Arsenal football club fans and much quieter, for a very simple reason: the monarchy, as Queen Elizabeth runs it, is the totem pole around which the satisfied tribe gathers contentedly. The British consider the royal family a good, old, reassuring habit.

Over the years the royal family has done its best to return the courtesy. It has allowed television in the Palace, journalists at the door and has supplied everyone with endless gossip. More importantly the British monarchy has never gone the way the Scandinavian or Dutch royalty has: the British love tradition, they would never have accepted a queen riding a bicycle. That does not mean that 'The Firm', that's what the Queen herself calls it, has not changed. What with weddings, children and squabbles, there has been no time to be bored. Many new developments have come about. For instance the young royals, Diana herself to start with, have a go from time to time at behaving exactly like 'any other young person', or Prince Charles decides to say what he thinks and is unfairly castigated by the tabloids. And what is more, the Queen was, until recently, saddled with a determined Prime Minister and a woman to boot.

The two women were of an age and of the two, the Queen was without any doubt the more loved and closer to the people, while Mrs Thatcher was more royal. She would use the 'Royal plural' ('we have become a grandmother'), and had gates installed at the end of Downing Street, just like Buckingham Palace. It could even be that they kept an eye on each other's wrinkles. But certainly the relationship between the two women was one of the most exciting British mysteries of the end of the century. The relationship may have been described as 'cordial', but it occasionally looked a bit too strained. There was a rumour that Elizabeth and Margaret did not get on at all: the British did not worry too much and gloated about it.

What we know for sure is that they had a tiff about clothing. There have been several instances when Mrs Thatcher was attending a ceremony in the presence of the Queen and the two women were wearing the same dress. After it had happened for the nth time, Downing Street discretely probed the Palace: was it possible for the Prime Minister to be informed of what the Queen was going to wear? From the Palace came a firm, polite refusal: Her Majesty was not in the habit of informing other ladies on the matter.

That story comes from John Pearson's book *The Ultimate Family* and is interesting as it casts some light on this silent battle. The two women were running the country and growing old together. The Queen was born in April 1926, and Mrs Thatcher in October 1925. Her Majesty has only been to 10 Downing Street once since Mrs Thatcher settled there. On the other hand they met every week at Buckingham Palace. In the two hundred and fifty years during which Prime Ministers have conferred with the Sovereign over the nation, it was the first time that two women have come face to face. There was a very precise ritual: at 6pm Mrs Thatcher's Jaguar left Downing Street, turned right at Whitehall, crossed Parliament Square and drove straight to Buckingham Palace. The Prime Minister was shown into the Queen's private study overlooking the gardens by a liveried valet. The meeting lasted an hour and was very informal.

There was mutual sympathy between the Queen and the two Labour leaders James Callaghan and Harold Wilson; Wilson even accompanied her on a visit to the Queen Mother: Her Majesty behind the wheel and the Prime Minister next to her sitting up straight. With Margaret Thatcher it was a different kettle of fish. She may have been the Leader of the Conservative Party, but she was too bustling and of the wrong class. It is said that after Grenada, the Queen kept Mrs Thatcher on her feet for the whole audience: Her Majesty had not been informed of anything and she was showing her displeasure. In November 1988 things went wrong again: apparently the Prime Minister was intending to veto a possible trip by the Queen to the Soviet Union. She apparently had an uncomfortable weekly meeting, whether sitting or standing history does not relate.

According to all the former Prime Ministers still alive, the Queen is incredibly well informed and she normally advises her advisers. Harold Wilson wrote: 'Her Majesty wanted to be informed of everything that was going on,' and Sir Alec Douglas-Home said: 'After over thirty-five years of reign, the Sovereign knows more than the diplomats who come to see her.' It is said that the Queen complained to the Foreign Office because their briefings were too 'elementary'.

Of all her different functions, the one the Queen cherishes most is 'Head of the Commonwealth'. She takes a great interest in the former colonies, which explains why the institution has survived the post-war years and its large number of Presidents, Generals and Dictators. When it comes to Commonwealth matters, the Queen does not follow any advice. She went to Ghana in 1961, in spite of Harold MacMillan preaching caution. In 1979, just after Mrs Thatcher's election, she was advised against attending a congress in Lusaka because of the war in Rhodesia. The press campaigned against the trip. The Queen listened to every one, said nothing and went. Her interest in British former colonies made for a difficult relationship with Mr Heath, the only 'European-minded' Prime Minister she has ever had. In the 1972 'Christmas address', which was delivered six days before Great Britain's entry into the EEC, the Queen bypassed the Prime Minister and informed the nation that entering into Europe did not alter 'the long-lasting and personal bond with our friends overseas'. In other words the European Community counted as much as the Commonwealth, possibly a little less.

The Queen, who is now over sixty, looks all her age: her mother aged better (at the age of ninety, the Queen Mother still enjoys icecreams on a gondola in Venice, that's why she is the most popular of all the royals). According to the experts, the Queen does not mind what she looks like: her style is to have no style. Her dresses are all the same, by the same Amies and Hartnell, and eventually stored in cupboards for an unspecified length of time. She used to have a taste for atrocious handbags in common with the Prime Minister, but Mrs Thatcher discovered dark suits and fashion. Because of her unassuming appearance and her strength of character, Elizabeth II is very popular. She introduced the walkabouts which the Princess of Wales subsequently elevated to an art form. It is said that her best achievement is to have persuaded her eldest son to marry a beautiful and unknown girl, and her second son to marry at all. Her daughter-in-law has become a super star: that does not worry her, it is good for 'The Firm'. But she was annoyed when at the 1984 opening of Parliament, the noble lords paid more attention to Diana's hairstyle than to her speech. Everyone agrees that under her careful management, the monarchy has become a perfect machine. It offers the crowds an alternative to American soaps – they are all there: the nice grandmother, the mischievous little sister, the wild son who eventually settles down – and on the other hand fascinates foreigners. To quote the *Boston Globe*: 'The British royal family comes out of ceremonies as the Israelis emerge from antiterrorist operations: with grandeur.'

Since the Queen is so capable–streetsmart according to an American diplomat – an abdication is very unlikely. There are many reasons for that: for a start the Queen herself pledged to the British that 'her whole life, whether long or short', would be spent at their service. The second reason is that the only time in British history that the monarch has passed the crown on to his son he was acting under duress: in 1327 a rebellion forced Edward II to leave the throne to his fifteen-year-old son, who became Edward III. The third reason is that she would become Queen Mother but there is already a Queen Mother, alive and well. There was only one chance of abdication according to some: if Mrs Thatcher had won the 1992 General Election, the Queen could decide to forget her pledges, history and her mother and steal the limelight.

But I am afraid now there is no chance of that, it would be too funny The Queen will stay where she is, and things will go on just the same: the British will go on admiring her in silence, while the popular press will carry on gossiping about the royal family, which they are terribly good at. This is what was fed to the nation on an ordinary Sunday: Prince Charles had grown tired of his wife and preferred to be with a young lady of gentle birth from Florence; Sarah had scoffed a mountain of strawberry jellys – Diana indulged in strawberry jelly when she was pregnant, ergo Sarah was pregnant; Sarah had said that at school she was the best at hockey, but she used to fall asleep during Latin; Prince Charles was the victim of a Jungian analyst who forced him to go for walks in the desert; Charles had wanted a black man amongst the guards at Buckingham Palace; he was in

Italy on his own, because his wife preferred English rock to Italian baroque.

When it grows tired of innuendoes and cannot invent anything new, the British press moralises. It is not only the quality press which might say something worth listening to, but the gutter press as well. The latter suffers from a form of schizophrenia: the front page features Princess Diana and all her sins, inside paternalistic editorials warn the royal family of the dangers of behaving like soap opera stars. It is normally the young royals who are the problem. Top of the list are the Princess of Wales and the Duchess of York. Prince Charles, on the other hand is hardly ever blamed for anything; he is looked at with wonder and bewilderment, especially since he started saying what he thinks about modern architecture, the environment and race relations, instead of smiling all the way to becoming Charles III, number 63 in the list of British monarchs.

The charges against Diana and Sarah go from the very generic to the very hysterical. The future queen and her sister-in-law were recently the object of an endless editorial in the *Sunday Times*. 'Charles and Andrew', it read 'have married two beautiful and fascinating women. But all too often their Sloane Ranger self takes over and they do not behave according to their rank, with disgraceful results.' In plain words, that means that Diana must not poke friends on their bottoms with the tip of her umbrella to attract their attention (it happened at Ascot, and he was a young banker by the name of Philip Dunne); Sarah must not split her sides, laughing and jump up and down like a clown (a reference to 'It's a Knock out', a charity show organised by Prince Edward, and also to her behaviour at Wimbledon); Diana must not show off her legs when entering her husband's Aston Martin, she must not drive around London on her own in the night and then zoom away at top speed when she is spotted, at the risk of causing an accident. Diana and Sarah should not dress up as policewomen and go to discos (it happened at Annabel's in Mayfair). Diana could at least pretend to like classical music as much as James Bond films.

That is all friendly stuff, but there are also heavy insinu-
ations and innuendoes, especially about Charles and Diana
themselves. Some time ago the normally well-informed
gossip columnist Nigel Dempster wrote that he had proof
positive that the princess had spent a week-end at the country house of a young family friend without his parents and
without her husband and Mr Dempster concluded apocalyp-
tically: 'There is fear and despair among the three thousand
people closely related to the Royal Family.' In 1987, for
the first time, eminent academics discussed in the press the
implications of a royal divorce. Books have appeared on the
subject as well, always disrespectful and normally published
in instalments in the Sunday press ('A match of opposites.
He does not understand her and apparently does not like
her all that much any longer,' said the *Sunday Times* across
a whole page). It is widely believed that they are two totally
different people: he likes painting, meditation and vege-
tarian cooking, she likes Sony Walkmans, shopping and
seaside holidays. When for the first time she left her husband behind at Balmoral – according to Anthony Holden,
author of *Charles: a biography*, she simply said 'Boring.
Raining'.

Only a few lone voices have spoken out against the excessive attention the media and publishers give to the Royal
Family. Professor Norman Stone, an Oxford historian, complained loudly against a 'Dallas-style monarchy' and advised
the Royal Family to be more remote, which according to
Bagehot, 'would help to preserve the magic'. But in spite of
his name, Professor Stone is not one of the Rolling Stones,
so no one listened to him.

Dreaming of the countryside

The 'Golden belt' stretches from Cornwall to Norfolk and includes Devon, Dorset, Somerset, Oxfordshire, Cambridgeshire and Suffolk. Whereas in the rest of the country the population in the last ten years has been stagnating, it has gone up 10 per cent there. In the past twenty-five years, in places like Dorset and Wiltshire the population has increased by a third and the number of dwellings by two thirds. Something strange is happening: the 'Golden Belt' is the English countryside, about which we have heard so much. Obviously an ever increasing number of Britons, after having spoken about it for decades, have decided that the time has come to go into the country and see for themselves.

This is no small phenomenon. According to Professor Howard Newby of Essex University the 'new rurals' are simply the vanguard of an army. For the first time since the Industrial Revolution, technological advances allow rural areas to compete on equal terms with the big cities. In other words, computer and fax machines, better roads, better trains and twenty-four-hour delivery services, make it possible to run a London job from rural East Anglia. Artists and professional people, writers and journalists have all come to the same conclusion and now they love being photographed in the colour supplements while they type away on their computers in the garden with their wives smiling at their shoulders and standing next to the barbecue.

In Great Britain the countryside is an ideal more than a place. All British people live in the countryside, at least in their imagination. Some fantasise about open fires in London, where they are forbidden by law, or dress in country casuals; some admire cows, fields and flowers in glossy magazines, thereby avoiding the showers and the muck.

The 'rural obsession' coincided with the time when British farmers started feeling the pinch, so they welcomed the new colonists with their packets of money and their boundless enthusiasm. The problems farmers are facing are rather recent: in the seventies they were doing well. But of late they have been hit by a series of bad harvests in staples like wheat and barley, and by the reform of the Common Argicultural Policy worked out in Brussels in 1988. In the last ten years there has been a steady 2 per cent-a-year reduction in the workforce and there are now very few rural districts where the proportion of the population engaged in farming is over a quarter. There are nowadays 260,000 farms in Great Britain, 70 per cent of which are run by their owners with a total workforce of 680,000. The Government is worried by those figures and has even encouraged farmers either to move into the tourist market or to sell their land to the specialists.

Just when farmers were having a rough time – it was not too bad though, British farmers, just like their continental colleagues, know how to milk the European Community – small businesses and service industries moved out into the country. Consequently unemployment in many rural areas has almost completely vanished and graduates are in very great demand, a state of affairs which exceeded Mrs Thatcher's wildest hopes. East Anglia – a flat landscape which reminds me of some parts of northern Italy – even managed to increase its manufacturing output between 1975 and 1985. Another pleasant surprise is to see how ready workers are to move from London or Birmingham: as soon as the transfer is proposed, off they go, delighted to settle in a sleepy Suffolk town where they can stroll on a Sunday in the market square and talk of the summer that never comes.

Ever since the invasion though, those sleepy towns are not so sleepy any longer. In Diss, in Norfolk, the population has doubled and in the High Street there are nine estate agents, busy making the best of the boom of the housing market, while it lasts. They are quite often responsible for rows upon rows of executives homes: big, cold, expensive houses with barren gardens and man-made slopes. The local residents, anxious 'for the view from someone's window', to quote an understanding Environment Secretary, discovered in horror that the building fever had hit the whole of the south: from East Essex to Gloucestershire, the overall volume of building increased by 60 per cent in the past ten years. The *Sunday Telegraph*, the most sensitive of all Sunday papers on this issue, lamented some time ago. 'It is now impossible to find a hilltop where no new ugly buildings are being planned; there is no place in England where the night sky is not spoiled by the orange lights of the expanding town.'

If you have not got the guts to go and colonise, you stay in London and dream. Those who can afford it – and many can after ten years of Mrs Thatcher – buy a weekend cottage. Many old families cannot come to terms with the crowds of new arrivals, their urge to build and the money they are prepared to cough up for a tumble down property. In the Cotswolds, for instance, gone are the charming, abandoned old houses typical of the English countryside: now every Friday night there is a traffic jam in the middle of Bourton-on-the-Water. The 'new-rustics' have come down to maintain their properties. Therefore the gardens which, according to the rural gentry, ought to look as natural as possible, are now absolutely spick and span with the help of a part-time gardener and of the young Mrs, who tells her friends back in town how she read Wordsworth to the hydrangeas.

Evelyn Waugh, who had meant *Brideshead Revisited* to be the swan song of the English country house and of the way of life that went with it, can be forgiven for not having imagined these new developments. Country houses suffered during Mrs Thatcher's reign but not as much as one thinks and not because of her: she only slapped heavy death duties on them. It is true that upkeeping costs have soared and servants have vanished, but the boom of the antique market has turned any old house into a gold mine. The sale of the contents of a couple of disused rooms – two oil paintings, six chairs, a couple of tables and a few odds and ends – can bring in the same amount of money as the value of the whole house fifteen years ago. Another clear sign of the changing times are all the works in progress around stately homes. In the old days only the roof used to get any attention at all, now greenhouses and tennis courts are springing up.

The revival of the countryside also has other consequences. A number of magazines, some of them recent, sell bucolic fantasies for just over a pound. *Country Living* has a romantic vision of the countryside focusing more on the curtain material than on the management of chickens. The magazine, which is in colour and printed on glossy paper, sells over 150,000. According to the Editor, Deirdre McSharry, the magazine has a clear role in the present as well as in the post-urban society to come. 'I cannot pretend to have any mud on my Gucci boots,' she says 'but I do believe that the countryside belongs to all of us, wherever we live. The countryside is a state of mind as much as a geographical location. It is far too important to leave it to farmers and politicians.' One would like to see what the farmers would say to that. *Country Homes and Interiors* is a bit along the same lines: 'Readers have no interest in geese and pigs, what they want are blazing log fires and long walks.' *Landscape* is another periodical of the same green hue. It recently merged with *Country Times*, the favourite read of people who love hunting and shooting. It will be interesting to see if the full-page adverts of the League Against Cruel Sports which *Landscape* used to carry, will stay.

If you do not read, do not hunt, live in a flat and are determined to be countrified, you decorate. The prices of country furniture have shot up recently. People have paid up to five thousand pounds for a gate-leg table after a pleasant chat with a satisfied dealer about its one and only drawer, the shape of the legs and the bad state of the hinges. Oak has almost overtaken mahogany in London dining rooms. Over week-ends young people in Barbour jackets – the waterproof invented by John Barbour in 1860 which is the perfect uniform of the outdoor gentleman – scour the Oxford countryside looking for craftsmen who specialise in mock Windsor chairs: after buying a period table they cannot afford the period chairs to go with it. In Gloucestershire at Stow-on-the-Wold, the bucolic longings of the nouveaux riches have created a new industry. The young owner of a tiny shop lit by two candles – no strip lighting in the countryside – confessed to tracking down antiques in a sportscar, with carphone and video equipment. When he comes across a good piece of country furniture – a Jacobean refectory table or a Charles II double gate-leg table which can seat twelve – he rings up his clients from the car and informs them that a videocassette is on the way. 'Well now,' we commented, 'this is America.' 'No!' was the answer. 'Americans pay much more.'

What is the mystery behind the wall paper?

Merridale Lane is one of those corners of Surrey where the inhabitants wage relentless battle against the stigma of suburbia. Trees, fertilised and cajoled into being in every front garden, half obscure the poky 'Character dwellings' which crouch behind them. The rusticity of the environment is enhanced by the wooden owls that keep guard over the names of the houses, and by crumbling dwarfs indefatigably poised over goldfish ponds. The inhabitants of Merridale Lane do not paint their dwarfs, suspecting this to be suburban vice, nor, for the same reason, do they varnish the owls; but wait patiently for the years to endow these treasures with an appearance of weathered antiquity, until one day even the beams on the garage may boast of beetle and woodworm.

John le Carré, *Call for the Dead*

In London, not far from Shepherd's Bush, lives a middle-aged married man, a very ordinary looking person, who worked for three years on his terraced house to restore it to its original state. He added window sills, restored brickwork, changed drains. When everything was ready he set up a spotlight in the garden and organised a 'son et lumière' for his neighbours. Then he succumbed to a nervous breakdown. The house, in spite of all the work that went into it, does not look any different to the untrained eye, but the owner is terribly proud of it. He is also convinced that he has increased its value and is pleased with himself for being a carpenter, plumber and craftsman rolled into one. It is quite likely that every evening on his way home, he looks up at his drainpipes, so much more beautiful than his neighbours', and feels pleased with himself.

The British suffer from a fascinating, highly commendable and deeply rooted obsession with buildings, which itself explains a lot of things. It is the reason for the surfeit of atrocious 'home improvements' articles in the Sunday supplements; for the £7.5 million a year turnover of the DIY industry; for the widespread practice of mortgages – possibly the widest used word in modern language – and also for the fact that after a murder, the papers give the price of the house where the body was found. 'A dead woman was found in the bathroom of her £250,000 Camden home', which means she is dead but she did not do too badly for herself when she was alive. The passion for the house explains the poorer aspect of Britain when compared to Italy, though the two countries have comparable GNP's. The British spend their money on an extension at the back, while Italians buy a car and park it in the front.

There are 22 million houses in Great Britain, a number of which are rather old: 3.5 million were built before 1880 and almost as many between 1881 and 1918. Four and a half million were built between the two wars and 7 million from the end of the Second World War to 1970. Only 15 per cent have been built in the last fifteen years, whereas in Italy 60 per cent of the housing stock is post-1960. The age of the house in which he eats, sleeps and watches telly, does not worry the average Englishman. He does not like new things; actually all manner of revivals (neo-classic, Tudor, baroque, gothic, Georgian, Byzantine) have been tried out to keep so-called modern architecture in check. When they tried something else they were severely punished, as we shall see further on.

The passion for detached small houses, which angered Roland Barthes so much, and fascinates you just as much when you fly over London prior to landing at Heathrow, is more rooted in people's minds than in their history. I do not think I can agree with Oliver Wendell Holmes when he says that 'the trouble with modern houses is that they have no room for a ghost', but I am sure that the British like to be alone and a small house sees to that: narrow windows, a small garden at the front, another one at the back and a hedge all around. Only in Britain, where borders are so important, could hedges supply inspiration to poets and students alike: John Evelyn, the great seventeenth century diarist, wondered whether 'there was anything more marvellous and relaxing under the sun, than an unpassable hedge' and Lord Keynes wrote just before the Second World War, that Britain's wealth was in its hedges, and with such hedges the country could face a long and expensive war with confidence. History proved him right.

The trauma for a country where people can just about cope with having two neighbours at a time to ignore, came in the fifties, when Queen Victoria's old rule – no house shall be taller than the firemen's ladders, nor wider than the street – was abandoned and programmes got under way to replace the 200,000 dwellings flattened by the Luftwaffe. A group of 'functionalist' architects with Le Corbusier in their heads, public money in their pockets and no maximum height restrictions went ahead with tower blocks, 'living machines' they called them. The first ones, for which the term 'concrete jungle' was coined, were on the Alton West Estate at Roehampton, a residential complex on the outskirts of London intended for 1,850 families. In 1964 the Labour Prime Minister, Harold Wilson, in order to keep his electoral promise of half a million new houses, authorised local authorities to proceed at full steam ahead. The results were not Victorian houses with windowboxes, but more tower blocks linked together with bridges, stairs and underground passages, with minute lifts, no parking spaces, no decent people to run them (the generation of retired navy officers, who had done the job in the fifties, had gone). The estates were hardly completed when the trouble started: leaks and cracks appeared on the walls, lifts were always out of order, vandals wrecked stairs and passages, while drunkards used them as public conveniences. Good neighbourly relations, which the project had wanted to foster, turned out to be pie in the sky. Just as they had done when they were living in individual houses, the British living in flats ignored each other, even on the other side of the landing.

Then came Ronan Point, Canning Town. At 6am on 16 May 1968, there was an explosion on the eighteenth floor, caused by an old lady switching on her oven. The whole block came down, five people died, eighteen were injured and that was the end of 'functionalist' architecture. A couple of years ago flats on the twentieth floor made a comeback and judging by the price fetched by penthouses at World's End in Chelsea, the trend is changing. In reality, the passion for lifts and rooms with staggering views is typical only of the wealthy intelligentsia. The other British, the real ones, still prefer the 'two up and two down', bow windows, white woodwork and an uncomfortable bathroom on the landing. Prince Charles, every time he talks about architecture, agrees with them.

The passion for their homes not suprisingly encourages many people to buy, instead of renting. Before the First

World War, nine out of ten families paid rent to private landlords. Now only three out of ten rent their homes, one from a private landlord and two from a Housing Authority of which there are 460 in Great Britain. These council house tenants looked forward to buying their property with the blessing of the ex-Prime Minister, who believed that people vote Conservative as soon as they become homeowners and they plan to change the wallpaper.

Wallpaper is not the only thing people like to play around with in their homes, as soon as they can legally do so. We have already talked about the annual DIY turnover. Let's add that in British houses there are 650,000 alterations and extensions under way year in year out. That is possible because, provided the building is not listed, the owner can do exactly as he or she pleases. The consequences of this laissez-faire attitude can be seen in some popular housing estates where the recent owners have gone wild with metal frame windows, stone cladding and mock Georgian front doors ('Kentucky Fried Georgian front doors' they are called in spite) for no other reason than to differentiate themselves from the tenants next door who still pay rent. In some instances the Local Council had to read the Riot Act to these DIY enthusiasts. So they unearthed a section of the General Development Order which allows them to appeal to the Environment Secretary. That happened in Wandsworth where the character of Totterdown Fields and of Dover House Estate, two of the best examples of popular housing dating back to the turn of the century, was under threat.

Sometimes, on the other hand, building work is indispensable: an important insurance company carried out a survey which concluded that 20 per cent of people who buy a house have to carry out expensive maintenance work within ten years of the purchase. This is a direct consequence of the ability of the 'conversion industry' to conceal flaws in old buildings. And they can fool the building society's experts as well. Foreigners are even more vulnerable: an employee of the Italian Cultural Institute had to get rid of his Holland Park flat after the ceiling simply collapsed.

When they are not busy converting, repairing or extending, the British decorate. The way they do it depends, of course, on their social position. The aristocracy goes about it absent-mindedly, buys no furniture, because it was passed down to them, mixes different styles in the same room, says 'drawing room' instead of 'living room', takes no notice of bathrooms and is surprised when anyone notices anything. 'Fellow noticed my chairs,' exclaimed the Earl of Derby when the visitor went away. The wealthy upper middle class takes a lot of trouble and spends a lot of money decorating, dipping into specialised magazines and copying from other rich people's homes, but cannot achieve the careless elegance of the aristocracy. This is upsetting, so they look for reassurance. Jilly Cooper, who wrote a very interesting analysis of British society, tells the story of a wealthy friend of hers who had asked an upper-class friend to her place to see her new interior decoration. He had put her down with a tart: 'Whatever for?'

The middle class behaves just as foreigners would expect it to: buys period furniture, lays patterned wall to wall carpets, has flowers all over the house, which could mean fresh flowers as well as plastic ones. The hallmark of the middle class used to be flock wallpaper, thick paper with red glistening lilies on a gold background. Now you can only find it in Indian restaurants out in suburbia, and some people go all the way there to look at it and touch it. The middle class is the most conservative and is very keen on revivals. Some revivals are more popular than others. Mock Tudor, for instance, with its exposed black beams, has never been abandoned. There are several reasons for that. Some say that the British love to go back to that period in history they know best and during which national identity was forged: the time of Henry VIII, Queen Elizabeth I, and Shakespeare. Other people think that since Britain was the first industrial country and the first country to suffer the consequences, it has been longing for the last century for a rural idyllic past, and that is better done under thick oak beams.

You cannot say that for a new group the wealthy upstarts – from rock stars to estate agents. They have been building ugly houses on the outskirts of London, with water beds, jacuzzis, burglar alarms and automatic doors which, thank God, no one can see as they are hidden behind tall perimeter walls. And finally to the working classes: enticed by advertising, they go for fancy water-closet covers, aluminium tables, fake Monets, holiday souvenirs from Spain, microwave ovens as big as television sets and television sets as big as aquaria. On the pinewood shelves are the book clubs' monthly deliveries and a glossy hardback on the Royal Family. Electric logs, which operate on a switch, have often replaced open fires in the fireplace. With the disappearance of flock wallpaper, they are now the symbol of suburban England. But I know of one lord who has electric logs and who switches them on when he is cold. But this does not prove anything: at home and outside, their Lordships do as they please.

Conclusion

Great Britain today is undoubtedly richer and more contented than in the early eighties, when it did not know what its place was in the world. Even those who cannot stand Margaret Thatcher agree that she administered the necessary medicine to the nation. And since nations, like children, do not like purges, she was not always popular. Thanks to her drastic remedies, the United Kingdom realised that it is not enough, at the dawn of the third millennium, to have been a great imperial power; today it is necessary to be a medium-sized European power. In the past years the country has woken up, sometimes painfully from the euphoria of winning the Second World War: like some members of the aristocracy, the nation has realised that it could not live on its laurels, but it had to set itself to work. Sometimes one has the impression it does not know which way to go about it, but that is another story.

The British are very keen to discuss the decline of the country – or as some think, the end of it. Entire sections of weekly magazines discuss the matter: 'Are we declining?' they ask. Everyone has a theory; it is a serious matter. Any cabbie can discuss the growth rate, industrial production, and the unemployment rate as incompetently as any politician. According to a recent poll, 80 per cent of the population thinks that law and order, morality, the English language and professional ethics, have all been declining in the last forty years. But the majority acknowledges that economic and industrial output, social integration and politics have all improved. Whether British politicians are any better than they used to be, is not something I am prepared to debate here: it would be too cruel for the Italian reader, who is accustomed to the antics of the Italian political class. As for social integration, I cannot agree: if the British car industry were as healthy as the class system is, we would all be driving Vauxhalls on the Continent instead of FIATs and Volkswagens.

The changes, the upheavals and being saddled with a woman Prime Minister have not altered the country deep down. The British still have qualities which are totally unknown to us: for instance, they respect the State, whether under the guise of a policeman or of a litter bin. Great Britain is a country where people may have untidy homes, but want clean streets: unlike some Italian families who are exceedingly fussy about their drawing rooms and throw the rubbish out of the window.

Another blessing is their passion for public welfare: top people end up in administration and are paid accordingly. There is less red tape: you can usually prove your identity with an address on an envelope. Laws were made for gentlemen and are therefore quite easy to evade, which a growing body of scoundrels have been only too quick to realise. Various stories in the City and the daily scandals in the housing market are there to prove it.

Another two national characteristics have not been altered: stoicism and thrift. The British put up with anything: rain, queues, wars, and they do not need much, judging by some of the plain decors of a number of British homes. Bagehot possibly had that in mind when he said that the British had one redeeming feature: they were stupid. It is an interesting observation: just look what sort of State we Italians, who think we are clever, have landed ourselves with.

Hypocrisy is another quality the British people have not shed. In all walks of life, in any class, the British choose to lie. Almost all of them, excluding perhaps the intelligentsia (there are other problems there), delight in obeying rituals and conventions, which flatter their inborn acting instinct. The polite forms in the English language are very revealing in this respect: the British telephone operator says 'Can I help you?' whereas her Italian counterpart hisses a curt 'Tell me' as if you were getting in her way.

The trouble with this courteous and educated nation comes when courtesy and education are not there. The British are not the same people when they are drunk, when they get angry, when they become fanatical. In the old days those 'qualities' helped them to win wars. Now drunkards, thugs and fanatics all go to football stadia and we know full well what they are capable of. Socially, these people belong to the middle and the lower classes. The middle class itself is reaching new depths of depravity, with the increase in child abuse cases and sex crimes. One almost regrets the days when its favourite form of crime was poisoning. The editor of the *Sunday Telegraph* the staunch Conservative, Sir Peregrine Worsthorne, wrote not long ago that all this is Mrs Thatcher's fault: she was the one who freed 'Homo Britannicus' from many constraints, without thinking that he could make bad use of his newly found freedom. Others have noted how surprised and grateful pedestrians are when a car stops for them at zebra crossings. This is new: until recently pedestrians crossed self-confidently, their heads high: they knew they were exercising their right. This is but a small symptom of a greater uneasiness: the country is rougher, solidarity and compassion have gone out of fashion, and people rightly or wrongly feel vulnerable.

Many people do not find their place in this New Great Britain which Mrs Thatcher has anchored to Europe and Mr Major will try to keep there. The old-fashioned Conservatives are totally lost. They used really to feel for other people's miseries and at Christmas they would visit tenants with blankets and boxes of biscuits. At the time of Concorde – a means of transport for which they have too much luggage and not enough cash – they were completely out of touch, and after ten years of Margaret Thatcher they were still wondering what hit them. The traditional left is even more in disarray: they have been preaching for twenty years to the poor and the angry, and they have watched their electorate turn their backs on ideology and reach for the video recorder. Only the middle class has emerged victorious out of the eighties: it seems perfectly satisfied with a bit more money to spend in those dull High Street shops. Some fear that Great Britain will look more and more like the States, to which Mrs Thatcher openly looked for inspiration. After having spent four years on the spot, I think this is quite unlikely: the people are too arrogant to copy anyone. And most of all they are too complacent: the mail gets there on time, beer is good and the Government not too bad.

Today Great Britain has won its greatest victory: not only has it a great past, but also a reasonable present. At long last, it is no longer the 'garden of eccentrics' we all loved to visit at least for a weekend, thinking we could understand everything and shrugging off with a laugh what we could not. By the way: we must not feel guilty about that. The British deserve to be examined in haste and judged without pity: for centuries they have applied that treatment to others in Europe and elsewhere. But they are quainter than they would like, and that is unforgivable.